Better BRAIN *Food*

Better BRAIN *Food*

Eat to cheat dementia and cognitive decline

NGAIRE HOBBINS APD, BSc, Dip Nutrition and Diet
Recipes by MICHELLE CRAWFORD

MURDOCH BOOKS
SYDNEY · LONDON

Contents

Foreword

We all want a healthy brain to help us stay engaged in life and achieving all that we hope for as we age.

Ageing is a triumph of modern medicine. Anyone now anywhere near their fifties or so will have had grandparents born close to the beginning of the twentieth century. Their life expectancy at birth was less than 70. Now we expect at least 10, more likely 20, years beyond that. Those extra years are a wonderful bonus but also impose unprecedented challenges to our bodies and brains: our lifestyles have changed. Some things we see as advantages — labour-saving devices and technologies, for example — are not helping our brains. They reduce our opportunities for everyday activity.

At the same time, many foods have moved further and further from their natural origins and that imposes changes in many ingredients that may impact the health of our brains. Science has shown that we need to embrace seasonal and local foods as much as we can, and combine them with colourful foods (a variety of colours — light, dark, strong and muted — indicate the presence of nutrients), brain-supporting oils and good proteins, for the sake of our brains.

The advice in this book is based on evidence uncovered so far by science about foods and ingredients that can help protect brain cells from damage, including damage due to oxidation and inflammation, and keep the systems that support them and their activities working as well as possible.

Despite the dire predictions you might hear, the majority of people living into their later years do not develop dementia: statistics indicate that approximately 10 per cent of people over 65 and 30 per cent of those over

85 are living with dementia, but that also means around 90 per cent of over-65s and 70 per cent of over-85s are not!

In this book you will learn the latest on all the ways you can help keep your brain healthy: lifestyle choices and activities that boost both physical and cognitive activity alongside brain-supporting eating strategies.

Science has not yet uncovered any one thing — food, gene or environmental factor — proven to prevent or cure the cognitive decline that can lead to dementia but it's reassuring to know about the things we can do to help keep our brains as healthy as possible and give us the best chance of avoiding disease. The recipes in this book are not only delicious, but offer inspiration for preparing meals to give your brain the best chance of peak health. Recipes are usually for two or more people, but guidance is also provided on adapting them to a single serve, to assist those cooking for just one.

In this selection of recipes, the focus is on including foods that provide ingredients thought to supply nutrients and other substances considered beneficial to the brain. These are delicious individual dishes, but they are not a whole diet. And remember, there is a lot more to good brain health than food alone. Lifelong physical activity and positive social interaction is paramount, supported by learning, thinking and planning throughout life and balanced by good sleep and regular meditative and/or religious practice to provide a bit of recuperative 'downtime'.

I am an Accredited Practising Dietitian: I hold a degree in science and my studies were in human health and physiology. I have postgraduate qualifications in nutrition and dietetics, more than 35 years of wide-ranging clinical experience in nutrition and, most importantly, my professional ethics mean I cannot, and will not, make claims unless I know there is enough medical evidence to back up what I say. The fact that I must answer to my professional association is essential: it protects people from unscrupulous claims and statements. Unless my views are supported by evidence from scientific study, I risk being disqualified as a dietitian and losing my professional credibility.

Our understanding of the contributing factors for brain health will continue to evolve and some advice may ultimately change, but that is the nature of medical research into the human brain. In this book I have taken a broad, practical approach, focusing on the areas in which advice is least likely to change very much.

NGAIRE HOBBINS

LIVING WITH DEMENTIA

A comment for people living with a dementia diagnosis and those who care about them:

There is absolutely nothing in the recipes in this book that precludes them from being prepared and enjoyed by people who are living with a diagnosis of dementia. The delicious recipes here incorporate foods and ingredients to help boost brain health and are of benefit to anyone, but they have generally been designed for people who are not living with this diagnosis.

My previous self-published book, *Eat To Cheat Dementia*, provides specific guidance and advice for people living with a diagnosis of dementia and those who care about them. It provides practical advice about the specific nutritional support

essential to hold off the rapid decline in health and the accelerated loss of ability that weight loss and malnutrition can too easily cause. It also discusses specific aspects of eating, such as the possible need for changes in the texture or types of foods offered and options to boost protein and energy in meals as necessary. The common eating challenges faced by people living with a dementia diagnosis, and guidance on how to best overcome them, is covered in that book.

My books are always firmly based on the latest scientific evidence and that continues to underpin the advice here. I choose language to communicate that to the everyday reader and cook and I stand behind every claim I make.

PART ONE

the Science

chapter 1

Feeding your brain

Almost every day there's another diet, rediscovered 'ancient' food or newly developed supplement powder or pill claiming to protect the brain and save you from dementia. Most of these promise a fairly quick-fix or simple strategy; the majority are aligned to one product or another, claiming to have an answer if you buy one product or another. It can be hard to know who to believe, but I encourage you to consider, when faced with enticing promises, who is making the claims and whether there might be commercial gain behind them.

Does the author have the qualifications to give advice in this area? Does what they say consider the complex interplay of factors at work in the brain and in human nutrition or include the broad range of research findings in brain health? Is there a pill, powder or single food or supplement behind the claims being made? The advice and the recipes in this book are based on scientific evidence and make no simplistic claims.

The body and the brain — and the way food can help or hinder the work we need them to do each day — are immensely complex. There is no simple picture and no simple answers to keeping your brain healthy. Anyone who tries to claim otherwise and provide advice accordingly, is either misguided or, more likely, trying to sell you something that will ultimately disappoint.

‘ **The key to brain health is not in any magic food or restrictive diet.** ’

When it comes to your brain, the way it performs at any stage of your life depends on everything that's been thrown at it day in day out, over the years. That includes your genetic make-up; your physical and mental activities; meditative and lifestyle practices; what you have eaten and done during all that time; as well as the impact of any sort of injury it has suffered: they all combine to determine the ultimate health of your brain.

The key to brain health, when it comes to food, is not in any magic food or restrictive diet, it's in the complex interplay of these myriad factors, including nutrition. There are hundreds of different nutrients — some are needed in greater quantities, some in just very small amounts — and the human body is truly incredible, being able to draw what it needs from the variety of foods we give it each day. You need to eat the right foods to provide the nutrients, but the ability of your brain and body to extract what each cell needs from everyday foods is outstanding. The marketers of supplements or the latest diets often fail to recognise those abilities, suggesting that you are unable to get by without the help of the product they are promoting. The old adage of 'if it seems too good to be true, it probably is' so often applies.

Scientists worldwide are working feverishly to understand what is really best for lifelong brain health. It is a challenging area of research because the brain is exceptionally good at self-protection: that's essential, given its immense workload, but it also makes it very difficult for scientists to learn the brain's secrets. It's only been quite recently that technology has allowed enough access to start to put together the puzzle of what might lead to cognitive decline and dementia.

Years ago, before we understood the human body and brain as well as we do now, snake-oil salesmen stood on street corners and spruiked their wares to passers-by. These were not people who had credible qualifications or who had spent years in professional practice; they were people who saw a market and often preyed upon fear to get people to buy their products. Things are not quite the same now, but technology gives people with similar aims access to a far wider audience. The virtual street corner of today's world and the scope of global marketing continues to throw up snake-oil salespeople in all sorts of guises.

Many are well intentioned, believing their diet plan or product is truly revolutionary; they might even quote scientific research to support their case. But they generally choose the research findings that suit their case and ignore the rest; their assertions may sound great, but when you look at the big picture, they don't always stack up.

They may be chefs or cooks, actresses or media personalities, sportspeople or lawyers, but the big difference — and what can be potentially dangerous to their followers — is that they don't have to answer to anyone: they can quote only the research that suits them, they can weave plausible pseudoscience tales

with charisma and confidence and say pretty much what they like. Some of that might be harmless and of little consequence to anything other than your wallet, but some could be harmful, especially to older people.

Before accepting advice, always do a bit of research: check the credibility, the nutrition qualifications (if any) and the accountability of anyone offering advice. Many high-profile promoters of diets or supplements will fall short in one or more of these areas.

> **' Giving up foods such as meat, dairy or grains can compromise nutrition, especially as you get older. '**

The fabulous thing about science is that we are always discovering new things. Sure, that can sometimes be frustrating when it seems advice keeps changing, but it's just adapting to new discoveries in a very complex area of research. In the area of brain health, there has been plenty learned about foods or ingredients that can help protect the brain. Research also uncovers foods or ingredients that show extra promise or seem to have special benefits. Sometimes these are promoted in marketing as superfoods or as part of the latest heavily promoted diet plan. Where these are discussed in the popular press or via social media, I have tried to give advice on a 'first do no harm' basis. If the science around them looks to have some potential benefit, even if it's not completely clear yet how or why that is, and their incorporation into recipes or eating plans can do no harm and just might help, they are discussed here. More evidence will emerge in time, of course.

Conversely, sometimes these same communication channels might have suggestions that certain foods need to be avoided to achieve benefits. But those restrictions might instead reduce an individual's access to valuable nutrients: giving up foods such as meat, dairy or grains can compromise nutrition, especially as you get older. Unless diagnosed with a specific need to avoid certain foods, it's important to take care and get good advice from a qualified professional before you choose to avoid them.

What you get in this beautiful book is a combination of the best of what science actually reveals about the foods that really support brain health, translated by Michelle Crawford into delicious meals, snacks and a few treats.

chapter 2

Understanding the brain

A brief summary of what we understand about neuroscience will give an insight into what's needed to keep the brain as healthy as possible.

The neurons

There are somewhere around 86 billion neurons in the brain, supported by between two and 10 times as many glial cells (see below), depending on the part of the brain you are looking at.

The neurons are the cells that do the communication: they receive messages from outside the brain, process that information, pass messages using specialised neurotransmitters and send messages back to the body to keep things running as they should and to keep us engaged in life.

If there are malfunctions in the neurons themselves; if blockages occur between them or message transfer is restricted in any way; if the ability to make specific neurotransmitters is hampered; messages can become confused or not get through at all.

This is extra-important because, while it is only about two per cent of your body weight, your brain consumes 20 to 25 per cent of the

energy and commandeers between 15 and 20 per cent of the blood flow in the entire body at any time: there is so much more going on per square centimetre in the brain than anywhere else in the body. It's impressive, for sure, but that fantastic level of activity also makes it extra-vulnerable to even tiny amounts of damage to neurons and the support systems around them.

That's where the glia come in.

The glia

Glial cells are the support system for the neurons, helping them receive the nourishment they need when they need it and performing a vital protective role by seeking out and helping rid the brain of substances that might harm neurons. They outnumber neurons in most parts of the brain, especially in those areas involved in learning, memory and conscious thought; in planning, personality and the management of complex skills. These are the areas in the brain where activity levels vary immensely, depending on what's going on in life, and it's here too where cognitive changes most often show up first. The greater activity capacity in these areas also makes neurons more vulnerable to damage, so the role of the glia in these areas is vital.

There are a few different types of glia (including astrocytes, microglia and satellite cells), with each group performing different roles, but I'm going to look at them here as a group. They help maintain good brain health in two main ways: the first has to do with blood flow through the brain; the second with their protective and resourcing role.

When it comes to blood supply, different areas of the brain demand very different amounts of resources depending on what they need to do at any time and so being able to increase blood flow to the areas that are active at different times is essential.

There is a large part of the brain that is always doing about the same amount of activity all the time, keeping all the processes that don't require conscious thought ticking along. If we had to actually think about taking every breath, producing digestive enzymes, processing an image sent in from the eyes or a sound from the ears, making hormones, causing a heartbeat or instructing the kidneys to filter our blood, we would have no time left for anything else in our day. The parts of the brain involved in this unconscious, everyday running of the body use around the same amount of fuel, nutrients and any other essentials each day and blood flow to the areas involved in these processes doesn't vary much as a result.

It's in the areas of the brain involved in conscious or 'non-automatic' functions that the glia truly get a chance to shine. These areas, where sense is made of complex information, have quite different needs to those involved in 'automatic' functions. Whether it's making new memories; thinking and planning; recognising and knowing how to manage and respond to words, sounds, images, faces and emotions; reading the newspaper; driving; learning a language; dancing; doing sudoku; practising tai chi; or just socialising and meeting new people, the areas of the brain that have to do all the complex processing to achieve those things — and more — must increase their activity massively. As a result, they need many, many more resources delivered immediately or you won't be able to keep up.

That's where the glia come in. They are able to significantly ramp up blood flow into areas doing extra work, giving express delivery of the nutrients, fuel and protective substances the neurons need. This is absolutely vital to our cognitive capacity. That is undoubtedly why there are more glia in areas that are involved in complex thought and planning activities than in parts that do more routine tasks.

The second area of support the glia provide is in provision of resources for and protection of neurons, and in seeking out and removing dead and damaged cells in the brain. Some glia produce the myelin that forms a protective coating around neurons.

To do all these things they, like all body cells, need to be resourced and supported. They can't fulfil their vital role unless they get everything necessary to run their activities. So everything you read in this book about fuelling, resourcing and protecting brain cells, applies to glia as much as neurons. As well, research suggests that omega-3 fats, including those from plant sources, are of special importance to the capabilities of the glia.

It's not possible to know, at this point in time, what comes first in declining brain health: does inflammation, oxidative stress or some other sort of damage in the brain cause glia to malfunction so that their ability to protect neurons is reduced? Or is there something about the glia themselves in some people that makes them less likely to be able to give the support the neurons need?

It's not yet clear, but as far as eating is concerned it doesn't really matter: in practical terms the glia and the neurons benefit from the same eating advice. The key is still in reducing the influence of possible brain-health negatives and maximising the positives, as discussed in greater detail in the following pages.

In time there will be medications or clear findings on specific strategies and individual substances that are able to assist glia should they be performing below par; for now the recommendations in this book can only help.

Brain-derived neurotrophic factor (BDNF)

It's worth mentioning here what researchers have learned just in the past few decades about the capacity of the brain to renew and repair itself. Until quite recently, it was thought that, if damage occurred to brain tissue, there was little or no way it could be repaired and the ability to achieve whatever that area would usually have been able to do, was lost forever. We now know that belief was wrong: the brain is able to develop new connections between neurons and to enlist the assistance of areas that may not usually do the work required. This is called 'neuroplasticity' and allows those who have suffered damage to the brain (through stroke or head injuries especially) to enlist other brain areas and make up for the loss of function that would otherwise result.

A substance scientists call brain-derived neurotrophic factor (BDNF) is one key player in neuroplasticity: it helps build the new connections between neurons and, excitingly, research suggests there are things we can do to influence its activity and production. Most powerful in this is exercise: any sort helps, but including bouts of higher-intensity activity is most effective, it seems. Regular exercise is also great for reducing stress, depression and anxiety, all of which might otherwise reduce BDNF activity. And balancing regular activity with meditative or relaxation activities is likely to help BDNF be more effective as well.

There could be some things in food that might help boost levels of BDNF and there are two things to consider: BDNF is a protein so it stands to reason that eating adequate amounts of protein, along with keeping a good reserve by maintaining body muscle is key to ensuring there are always adequate amounts of nutrients available to make BDNF when required. Beyond that, the capacity of food to assist is discussed in the next chapter.

The second thing to mention is that most of the research you might read has usually measured levels of BDNF in the blood, mostly because that's a lot easier to do than taking samples inside the brain, and scientists are not exactly sure how levels of BDNF in the blood relate to levels inside the brain, because the blood–brain barrier restricts their movement.

More will be revealed as technology advances our understanding of the brain, but it stands to reason that anything that increases BDNF levels in the body will probably have a close association with what's happening in the brain.

The blood–brain barrier

The blood vessels in the brain are different to those in the rest of the body in that they are surrounded by a layer of specialised cells that act as a barrier between what's in the blood and the highly vulnerable, but also highly demanding, brain cells. This blood–brain barrier is an important extra layer of protection, but does provide some challenges when it comes to getting some substances into and out of the brain.

Some things brain cells need, such as glucose for fuel and amino acids (the building blocks of proteins) for BDNF and neurotransmitters, get across the barrier with the assistance of special 'carrier' systems; a few substances are small enough to slip through themselves; but most are blocked. Different nutrients use different carrier systems: the brain fuel, glucose, uses a different system to that of amino acids. But some substances need to share carriers.

Interestingly, the substance that builds up in the brains of many people with Alzheimer's dementia, *beta* amyloid (Aβ), uses the same transporter to get out of the brain as a breakdown product of the hormone insulin. In insulin resistance, there is more insulin in the blood, and therefore the brain, than usual and, as with all substances the brain uses, it needs to be removed when its work is done. So if the carriers are loaded with insulin breakdown products on their way out of the brain, it is thought the capacity to remove excess Aβ might be reduced. In that way, insulin resistance might encourage the accumulation of Aβ in the brain, ultimately resulting in the plaques seen in Alzheimer's disease.

Another area of research has suggested that problems may develop in the blood–brain barrier many years before cognitive decline is evident that make the barrier 'leaky'. Substances that would otherwise be excluded from the brain for its protection can slip

through. This could be a consequence of age to some extent, but there is gathering evidence that obesity in early or middle adulthood is a significant contributor. It's still quite early days in this research, but the advice — little different to the rest of this book — would again be to do all you can to reduce excessive weight, if you are overweight in early and middle adulthood, and stay active throughout life to boost muscle and help your brain.

The blood–brain barrier, as discussed below in the section on neurotransmitters, also affects the production of individual neurotransmitters inside the brain, therefore potentially influencing cognition. That is because amino acids, from which neurotransmitters are produced, have to be transported into the brain with the assistance of special 'carriers' and they can limit the rate at which individual amino acids get through.

The neurotransmitters

There are as many as 100 or so different substances that can be called neurotransmitters (though about 10 do most of the work) and they are made in the brain from various substances that all need to be transported across the blood–brain barrier. They are also made by bacteria residing in the gut and in the gut wall.

You might read on the internet or in the popular press about foods (or supplements) that make the claim to boost levels of certain neurotransmitters. While it is true that different neurotransmitters are made from specific amino acids (the basic units of proteins), the carriers don't individually select which amino acids they take. Instead, they move whichever one gets there first; so, even if we wish one neurotransmitter

could be produced before another, it won't happen until the specific amino acid that that neurotransmitter is waiting on gets through. There are 21 amino acids, but only a few are needed to make neurotransmitters, and most are used in other ways in the brain. It doesn't seem that it is as easy as some claim to influence production of specific neurotransmitters by eating different foods; not surprisingly, it is much more complex than that. For most people, it's best to eat a variety of foods to give the brain access to what it needs.

It is worth taking a bit more of a look at the most common neurotransmitters, but there is a very long way to go to really understand exactly how, and if, what we eat can influence them.

> **' We do know that depression is linked in some way to dementia. '**

Serotonin is the neurotransmitter that is said to help give a positive outlook on life and reduce levels of anxiety and stress. It's also associated with a more 'calm' gut function: anxiety and gastrointestinal upset are well recognised as being related, and that interplay is part of investigations into the gut–brain axis described further in Chapter 6.

Depression is associated, among other things, with low levels of serotonin; the most commonly prescribed antidepressants, the selective serotonin reuptake inhibitors (SSRIs) work to boost levels in the brain. And serotonin also has roles in memory, learning, sleep, social behaviour and many more things of importance in brain health.

This is potentially important because we do know that depression is linked in some way to dementia: scientists looking at the brains of people who had passed away found lower levels of serotonin in the brains of people with Alzheimer's disease than in those of people who hadn't had Alzheimer's. And while that doesn't tell us if Alzheimer's causes reduced production of serotonin in the brain or if low levels of serotonin somehow contribute to Alzheimer's, it is certainly a reason to treat depression and reduce the chance that it may contribute to the development of cognitive decline and dementia.

Serotonin and some other neurotransmitters have received a lot of attention in recent years because they are not only made in the brain, but also in special cells that line the gut and by some gut bacteria. Serotonin is made from the amino acid tryptophan and its production in the gut wall is assisted by other substances produced by bacteria in the gut. It is not possible for serotonin produced in the gut to get into the brain directly, as it can't cross the blood–brain barrier, but tryptophan and other substances produced from it in the gut can, so that serotonin can be made inside the brain. As well, the same cells in the gut wall that produce neurotransmitters, including serotonin, also form a communication link between the gut and the brain via the vagus nerve. It is via this nerve that researchers believe the gut bacteria are able to influence brain health and vice versa. Read more about the association between a healthy gut microbiome and brain health in Chapter 6.

The neurotransmitter *gamma*-Aminobutyric acid (GABA) supports, and is said to 'calm', the nervous system, playing a critical role in mental alertness, elevated mood and avoiding depression. GABA is made from the amino acid glutamic acid with assistance from vitamin B6 and is also produced by gut bacteria.

The brain's reward and pleasure centres are largely controlled by the neurotransmitter dopamine, which is made in the brain from the amino acid tyrosine, and it also helps control movement in the body as well as emotional responses. Its regulation of competitiveness and aggression has probably made us successful as humans. This is the neurotransmitter impacted in Parkinson's disease, where inadequate supply causes movement issues, but can contribute in time to a type of dementia. In contrast, an oversupply (which happens when taking some illicit drugs, particularly methamphetamines) causes severe aggression and euphoria.

Norepinephrine (or noradrenaline) is involved in heightening body and brain activity levels and awareness. It's also important in embedding memories; in other words, holding onto things seen or experienced so they stick around to be recalled later. It is manufactured from tyrosine, in another step along from dopamine in the production process.

It might seem, reading the popular press or perusing the shelves of health-food stores, that the actions of single neurotransmitters are distinct and you can take supplements that will alter the levels in the brain and bring about certain effects, such as improved mood or better sleep. In reality, unless you have a diagnosed deficiency or imbalance, your mood, cognitive abilities and long-term brain health rely on the complex, combined interplay of the actions of all the different neurotransmitters.

The blood vessels and glymphatic system

That brings us to the blood vessels: about a quarter of the blood pumped out of the heart at any time is flowing through the brain, delivering oxygen, fuel, fluids and nutrients so it can do its work. The blood vessels need to be in absolute peak health to be able to do this, as well as to accommodate those massive variations in blood flow discussed earlier in this chapter. Anything that hampers that flow can affect the brain's capacity. Blockages in blood vessels cause cells supported by them to die: that's what happens in a stroke. But even the slightest restriction to blood flow will also potentially restrict the capacity of brain cells to achieve what they need to, and importantly might also reduce the access of protective substances to those cells. Blood vessels stiffened or restricted by inactivity and poor diet over many years, combined with even tiny amounts of damage that have accumulated over that time, can add up and eventually contribute to cognitive decline.

The blood also supports the glymphatic system. This is an active waste-removal mechanism specific to the brain that has only recently been discovered by scientists. With the brain being so much more metabolically active than any other part of the body, the glymphatic system is necessary to remove the wastes of all that activity, stopping them building up inside cells. An efficient blood flow helps keep that system running smoothly, too.

It is thought that intermittent blood-flow restriction over many years, even if it doesn't cause cells to die, might cause damaging changes in brain cells that eventually make them less able to fuel or protect themselves — naturally that will impact the brain's abilities in the short term, but in time can also lead to cognitive decline and dementia. It is well known that fuel use in areas of the brain affected in dementia is reduced and inefficient blood flow through the brain is one factor that might contribute to that.

chapter 3

What you can change

There are many factors other than diet that influence brain health: making lifestyle changes where you can is important. Where possible, improve your brain's chances of staying healthy by increasing physical activity; maintaining social connections; practising relaxation; seeking learning opportunities; and avoiding brain injury.

Fighting gravity and staying physically active

Let's be quite clear here, this is a book all about food, but no matter how important that is in brain health, *nothing* is as powerful as regular physical activity. It does so many things to boost brain health:

- it maximises blood flow through the brain as well as the body, helping get nutrients, fuels and oxygen to brain cells.
- it helps in the production of brain-derived neurotrophic factor (BDNF), which builds and supports both new and old connections, increasing brain plasticity so it can adapt in the face of any injury. Any exercise (higher-intensity activity might work best) seems to help production of BDNF.

- it assists with glucose metabolism and diabetes management and reduces insulin resistance. This is important because diabetes is associated with a higher incidence of dementia, thought to be mostly related to insulin resistance (you can read more about this in Chapter 7). The more regular exercise you can do, the better your ability to use insulin (whether that be what you produce naturally if you do not have diabetes, or what you receive via a medication or injection). In other words, reducing insulin resistance helps your brain.
- it increases levels of mood-enhancing (and therefore positive to brain health) neurotransmitters.
- it greatly reduces chronic inflammation – you can read more about this in Chapter 5.
- it gives the whole brain a work-out by bringing into play all the different systems from many areas in the brain that are needed to keep your walk, golf game, bike ride, dance class or gym session planned and coordinated — from memories of technique, rules, strategies and the like to managing muscles, balance systems, and all the senses needed to see, hear and feel those activities.

Social connection, meditative practice and brain downtime

Your brain needs a combination of lots of things to do, with time in between to rest and recoup. Research clearly shows that social connectedness is very good for the brain: chatting, interacting with old and new faces, negotiating all the nuances of good manners and expectations. All of these and more keep neurons in the brain firing, maintaining existing as well as forging new connections; however, it needs rest. Anything you do that allows a bit of time away from complex thought is good for your brain. It doesn't matter if that's going for a run, having a game of golf or paddling a kayak, prayer, meditation or Gregorian chanting — anything you can do to help your brain 'switch off' or focus on just one thing in a quiet way is important.

Cognitive reserve

Every day, life gives the brain myriad opportunities to build more and more networks between neurons. That does more than just keep us functioning in our world. Every new experience, every challenge mastered, every skill practised and honed, all the ways we dare our brains to do new things, forces it to set up more and more complex internal networks, making more and more connections between individual cells. The more connections brain cells make throughout life, the more you amass what is called 'cognitive reserve'.

It's like a well-stocked pantry and freezer: if you can't get out to shop when you'd like to, you still have plenty available to make yummy meals. And the greater the number of different things you have in stock, the more varied your meals can be and the longer you can hold out before you go hungry. If there is not much there to start with, you will struggle much sooner. You don't want your brain to 'go hungry', so you need to do all you can to stock the pantry and freezer, and keep it that way. That's especially important as you age. The more you stock your brain 'pantry' with experience, learning, practices and activities, the bigger the network of connections — the cognitive reserve — that will keep it from going 'hungry' and not being able to do what you need of it to keep your life on track.

A greater cognitive reserve provides the brain with more space to adapt if connections are lost at one point or another. The more experience you can give your brain at any age, both physically and mentally, the better chance you have of weathering any such problems later on, should they occur.

> ❛ The more connections brain cells make throughout life, the more you amass what is called "cognitive reserve". ❜

It's never too late to add to your cognitive reserve: brain training exercises, crosswords, sudoku, brain games and the like are all great, but do try to mix them up a bit — you need to add new activities and learn new skills now and then to get the best benefits.

Doing interesting things, interacting socially and learning new skills does much for your cognitive reserve, and people who have a good cognitive reserve are able to maintain their usual daily activities and get more from life for longer, once they suffer some sort of cognitive decline.

chapter 4

Eating to prevent dementia

Everything your body is and everything it does relies entirely on food. The nutrients we eat build cells, create organs, bones, muscles and the brain. They also supply everything needed to keep our bodies running, provide security and protection, and do any repair work.

Within the brain, nutrients supplied by food make neurotransmitters for communication, maintain all the support systems for neurons and glia for every bit of work they do, and provide fuel so cells can function and are able to mount the protection they need to keep themselves healthy.

It's extremely complex stuff and many people fail to recognise that our bodies and brains are immensely impressive: nutrients are sorted through and directed to the place they are needed minute by minute, day by day. Most of the time we don't really need to help them do that; we manage to get around, to work, to play, think, love and plan — all on whatever we happen to put in our mouths. But modern life offers challenges that threaten to stop us in our tracks. Eating the right combinations of foods can help us deal with those challenges.

This becomes all the more important because of the extra years we can expect to live. There will always be things we eat and do, or that are the usual consequences of day-to-day cell activity, that can potentially damage our cells, but since we are routinely living decades longer than the generations before us did, the chance that these effects might build up and cause damage increases with each passing year.

Our bodies and brains have an array of excellent defence and repair options available to them, but it stands to reason that the longer we live, the more possibility that otherwise insignificant amounts of damage might add up.

❛ There is *no one food* that supplies everything the brain needs to function at peak capacity. ❜

There is a common misconception when it comes to the brain that we need to eat specific foods to supply certain individual nutrients to help it function; but in reality, as long as the basics are made available it can draw what it needs. What's more, it's impossible to know what the brain might need at any moment, so the greater the variety of foods eaten, the better the chance that you will cover all bases.

No matter what you hear widely touted about the latest 'superfood', no matter how absolutely packed it is with vital substances such as antioxidants or vitamins, there is *no one food* that supplies everything the brain needs to function at peak capacity. Protection of super-sensitive and fragile brain cells is of course essential, but unless the fuel and nutrients to keep everyday activity and maintenance going are also available, your brain might not work as well as you'd hoped.

Supply and demand

Anything that is good for your heart is also good for your brain. All this talk of nutrition and brain health might seem a bit new, but that's not the case with heart health: it's been a high-profile topic for decades. It's well accepted that eating plenty of vegetables, fruits and fibrous foods is a good strategy for your heart. That goes along with keeping your weight down, especially when you are young.

Of course it makes sense that the heart and brain are linked: the heart pumps blood and blood transports nutrients from food, and oxygen from the air, to the brain. If blood flow is hampered in any way, those things might not make it to where they are needed.

Blockage in the blood vessels supplying the heart muscle causes a heart attack; if the blockage happens in the brain, it is a stroke. The cells that die following either event can't readily be recovered, although the brain can adapt through neuroplasticity, by making new connections between cells and enlisting other brain areas to help take on functions that might have been lost as a result.

The effects of intermittent, temporary or partial restriction to blood flow over many years are also important to long-term brain health. These factors are now thought to be part of the picture in some types of dementia. A single instance of cell resources being reduced and toxic waste products allowed to hang around brain cells longer than they should is probably of little consequence, but over decades if those instances are repeated, the effects add up.

‘ Anything that is good for your heart is also good for your brain. ’

Patterns of food intake that are good for your heart are therefore also good for your brain: there has been discussion for decades around the best diet for heart health and most often a Mediterranean-style eating plan is advanced. It's also more recently been widely accepted as being helpful for brain health. You can read more about this and other diet plans thought to help heart and brain health in Chapter 8.

Brain fuel

There is often a lot of talk about antioxidants or omega-3 fats or all sorts of other nutrients that might help brain health — and they do, of course — but what can't be overlooked is the fact that the brain can't achieve anything unless the neurons and the glia are supplied with the fuel that they need to keep everything running.

Research supports this, showing that fuel use is reduced in the brains of people with dementia; and probably has been for some time before the diagnosis is made. At this stage it is not clear which is the cause and which the effect. There may be some sort of malfunction in the cells causing them to underuse fuel, resulting in a gradual accumulation of damage over the years; or perhaps damage has accumulated due to other causes and that makes cells unable to use fuel efficiently. Whatever the answer turns out to be, however, it highlights the necessity of efficiently fuelling cells in the brain as the foundation for good brain health.

Fuel for your brain comes almost exclusively from glucose. Remember that, although it is only about two per cent of your body weight, the brain is so metabolically active — a medical term for being really 'busy' — it uses up a whopping 20 per cent or more of your body's total energy supply.

Some parts of the brain tick along, keeping all the background body systems running — things like breathing and digesting and keeping the heart beating and body organs functioning — and these use a fairly constant amount of fuel; however, activity in the areas involved in cognition — the thinking processes of the brain: planning, analysing, observing and making sense of things — fluctuates massively depending on what you are doing at any moment. At peak times the demand for fuel is extremely high so even minor blockages in supply are going to reduce cognitive ability.

There are three main things to consider when it comes to fuelling the brain:
- where the glucose comes from: foods and body stores.
- the ability of brain cells to obtain and use glucose effectively when it is available in the body.
- the possibility that the brain's fuel supply could be boosted in some other way if glucose use is down.

Muscle supporting the brain

Glucose for the brain comes from carbohydrate-containing foods (sugars and starches) and from very limited body carbohydrate reserves. When these sources are used up, protein is released from muscle and converted to glucose to boost supply. This protein reserve kicks in for most people after about a day with little or no food intake. If you are unwell, or if your food intake is low for other reasons, it could play a bigger part sooner. For anyone who is below middle age, this is of little consequence because body systems are set up to quickly replace muscle losses from protein eaten at the next meal, but beyond that age, changes in body physiology that are a consequence of the advancing years mean the muscles are only efficiently replenished when they are challenged with physical activity and provided with adequate protein in meals.

' Although it is only about two per cent of your body weight, the brain is so metabolically active, it uses up a whopping 20 per cent or more of your body's total energy supply. '

The ability to get glucose from the reserve of protein held in the muscles is ideal because for most of our lives we have far more muscle than we use every day. But that changes as people age. In older people, food (especially protein) intake and activity levels can fall. That combines with loss of muscle protein reserves due to age-related changes in body physiology and a reduced capacity to replace such losses, so that a time may come when the reserve is not adequate. This loss of muscle can eventually impact not only brain function, but also immune system effectiveness, body organ maintenance and wound repair, as well as physical function.

The best carbohydrates for brain fuel come from starchy vegetables, grains, pulses, dairy foods and fruits — and they have the added advantage of providing a variety of other important nutrients. Protein needs to be included, too, to keep the muscle reserve up. Dairy foods and pulses like lentils, chickpeas (garbanzo beans) and soya beans are excellent because they supply both protein and carbohydrate, but a meal with a concentrated protein food — such as meat, eggs, chicken or fish — as well as lots of vegetables, grains and fruits is also ideal.

For older people, maintaining muscle is essential so protein foods become more important to assist in that: I always recommend that there should be a protein food at the centre of every meal. As discussed further in Chapter 9, it's the combination of protein from food and muscle activity that is what works, so maybe that advice needs the addition of 'do some exercise with every meal'!

Sugars are carbohydrates too and are also sources of brain fuel, but eating too much added sugar in drinks, snack foods and recipes should be minimised, especially for younger people where it adds kilojoules without any other useful nutrients. This is important when it comes to reducing the impact of inflammation, as you will read in Chapter 5.

There is immense advantage in eating foods in their most 'natural' form possible: adding sugar to foods can be useful in preservation, but more often nowadays it is simply another step in processing, when those foods are best eaten in their natural state. Having said that, though, sugar in the occasional cake or dessert — which, let's face it, obviously should not make up your whole day's eating — is of little consequence. The glucose the brain needs can as easily come from starches in vegetables, grains, dairy foods and fruits as from sucrose, honey, malt or other sugars.

When it comes to older people — particularly those in whom appetite is reduced or who are frail — the inclusion of sugar in recipes or the consumption of foods containing added sugar can actually be helpful. Sugar is enjoyable and in people who are becoming frail, it can be a very useful way to entice, encouraging eating and adding extra appeal to foods that also provide essential nutrients. Not only that, it also provides easily accessible glucose for brain cells; diets that try to avoid sugar might in fact be unhelpful to the brain health of older people for that reason.

> **' For older people, maintaining muscle is essential so protein foods become more important. '**

So glucose is being supplied, but that's just one part of the story; getting it into the brain cells is entirely another. Unless that happens efficiently, the brain doesn't get fuelled efficiently either, and the process to get it there is quite complex. It involves the hormone insulin, along with the combined actions of its own specialised carriers to move glucose across the blood–brain barrier. The important role of the glia in causing the extra blood flow, covered in Chapter 2, is vital to deliver more glucose and other resources where and when they are needed.

Insulin works throughout the body and brain predominantly by assisting glucose to get into cells. In insulin resistance, a condition usually, but not always, associated with obesity and type 2 diabetes, cells do not accept the glucose as readily as they should — they have become resistant to the insulin. The consequences are many, but what is relevant here is that despite there being plenty of glucose in the blood (in fact, too much!), the cells don't get what they need. So, in those areas of the brain involved in complex thought and cognition with very high but intermittent fuel demands, insulin would usually give a glucose boost to brain cells; however, with insulin resistance, that doesn't happen as it should, creating big problems for the brain and reducing its ability to get the glucose it needs where and when it needs it most. You can read more on diabetes and brain health in Chapter 7.

❛ Diets that try to avoid sugar might in fact be unhelpful to the brain health of older people. ❜

At this point, it is important to know that your muscles come to the rescue again: they help your brain out when it comes to insulin resistance and type 2 diabetes because active muscles are able to use up excess glucose in the blood, helping keep both blood glucose and insulin levels down.

Remaining physically active throughout life and doing any exercise you can manage will help reduce insulin resistance and maintain body muscle. In younger adulthood, loss of any excess body weight by combining a sensible diet with activity is essential to reduce associated chronic inflammation as well as minimise the impact of diabetes and insulin resistance.

At a later age, weight loss and eating too little, by contrast, cause loss of muscle that

increases the chances of a diagnosis of type 2 diabetes or insulin resistance, or worsen those in people already diagnosed, while also denying the body a healthy protein reserve.

Glucose boost

If there are problems with glucose use in the brain, is there a way to use different fuels, or to boost the use of glucose with food? There may be: it seems that omega-3 fats have a role to play in fuelling the brain. They can't be used as fuel themselves, but one in particular — docosahexaenoic acid (DHA) from fish and other marine oils (food sources at the end of this chapter) — helps the neurons access and use glucose as well as assisting the brain in many other ways. The brains of people with Alzheimer's disease not only use less glucose, but also have been found to have lower levels of DHA than those without Alzheimer's, so it's very likely they are linked, although it's not exactly clear how yet.

Two other omega-3 fats also seem to be important: *alpha*-Linolenic acid (ALA), and eicosapentaenoic acid (EPA) — see the end of this chapter for food sources — are both involved in bolstering fuel supply to cells either by supporting glucose availability, or by boosting ketone supply (read on for more about this) for times when glucose just isn't in adequate supply. ALA can also be converted to DHA to increase its availability.

You may read that ALA conversion to DHA is insignificant, and some research in recent years has supported this. But other work indicates that it might depend on how much DHA is in the food you eat. For people who get enough DHA by eating oily fish, meat or milk from wild or pasture-fed animals, or from taking fish-oil supplements, the rate of conversion of ALA to DHA seems to be low. But in those who only eat plant foods and thus get no DHA in their usual foods, it seems ALA conversion to DHA is higher. That does seem to be plausible since vegans and others who eat almost no DHA, but get plenty of ALA from plant foods, don't necessarily end up with low brain DHA levels or dementia.

Backup fuel

Remember that glucose will *always* be the brain's preferred fuel, but the brain is able to employ some strategies to access backup fuel in unusual situations when the glucose supply is inadequate: it can use substances called ketones. However, managing to supply ketones to brain cells is not without challenges, so the contribution this alternative fuel is able to make remains low.

In people already living with dementia or cognitive decline and in whom, therefore, it can be reliably assumed brain fuel use is lowered, being able to offer an alternative to glucose, or something that can boost its availability, is certainly appealing to help maintain independence and cognitive capacity longer. That thinking has led to the promotion of 'ketogenic' diets (eating foods that increase the production of substances called ketones) by some people.

Before you read on, however, be aware that there is not a lot of evidence that this works for most people already diagnosed with dementia, and there is no evidence that boosting brain fuel use with ketones can *prevent* cognitive decline or dementia.

You don't get ketones from food and they are not available through the simple conversion of usual food components in the same way that glucose is: ketones are made by the liver from body fat or fat in food, after that has been broken down into fatty acids (fat's smallest components), but until recently we believed that mostly only happened when a person was starving (and that means actually starving, not just exaggerating feelings of hunger!).

During starvation (or in extended fasts or extreme 'ketogenic' diets designed to mimic starvation) the liver swings into action, converting fatty acids stored in body fat reserves into ketones that can be used by fuel-hungry brain cells, as well as in the rest of the body.

This is great because the brain can work well with ketones as a supplementary fuel, but — and here is where the proponents of this type of eating for brain health can come unstuck — that's only going to happen if starvation is affecting the whole body. Unfortunately, it doesn't happen just because some cells in the brain are, for whatever reason, underutilising glucose. In general, the sort of starvation that really boosts ketone levels enough to be able to influence brain activity levels is not what you would get from an overnight fast, a day or so of not eating due to illness or even what results during intermittent fasting-style diets or during religious fasting practices; and it is certainly not something that would be of benefit to anyone beyond their mid 60s, or anyone with dementia, mostly because one consequence will be unhealthy loss of body muscle reserves in these people.

So researchers have been looking at other ways they might be able to get the body to produce ketones to support brain cells that are not being fuelled adequately, without having to starve people. That means either getting

the liver making more ketones than it would usually, or finding another way to supply them.

It was with great anticipation that researchers started to look at using these diets to boost cognition in people with cognitive decline and dementia. But the findings haven't been as good as was hoped and these strict ketogenic diets are not easy for anyone, let alone someone living with dementia, because they are too unusual and challenging to manage most of the time.

The use of a type of fat called medium-chain triglyceride (MCT) has been part of that. This is a really interesting type of fat because it's able to bypass conversion into fatty acids so can be made directly into ketones; therefore it was thought that might be a big plus when brain glucose use was down. This type of 'modified ketogenic diet' doesn't require the severe restriction of carbohydrate foods that would usually be needed in a ketogenic diet, so it is easier to manage. There has been some evidence that this does help some people, although unfortunately that result is not as universal as was hoped.

Most MCT therapeutic diets use a commercially made product; however, coconut or coconut oil (which is now widely marketed in organic, virgin and all manner of other forms and is also known as copha in cooking) is an abundant source of MCTs in natural food. Manufacturers of MCT oils and coconut products have widely promoted the benefits of the MCT–coconut oil diet in treating dementia, even claiming preventive effects, but unfortunately the science isn't as encouraging as the marketing claims.

There has been a small number of people who have found that a coconut oil-based diet has helped them and they have received a lot of publicity, but sadly there are many, many more who have not gained benefit and we don't tend to hear from them. People marketing coconut oil naturally promote any success stories and we can easily get the impression that this diet is the answer to brain health. But researchers have been looking at this for a while now and they haven't found the benefits that are widely claimed.

It is my own opinion that some of the benefits seen are more the result of paying attention to eating than of coconut oil as such: inadequate food intake, weight loss and malnutrition are common and impose a heavy toll on physical and cognitive capacity in cognitive decline and dementia. Getting enough coconut oil or MCT oil into a daily eating plan requires dedication: a strong focus on meal planning around those ingredients because they are hard to eat alone, as well as encouragement of food intake, and those things are of immense benefit in themselves.

For someone diagnosed with dementia, there is no harm in trying coconut oil, as long as gastrointestinal upset is avoided by building up slowly to the approximately three tablespoons recommended per day. If it helps maintain or improve quality of life, it is a bonus.

However, for everyone else, there is no evidence from the science at this stage that a high intake of coconut oil is of benefit to brain health in the long term. The best advice, well supported by the scientific evidence, is that glucose availability to brain cells will be boosted by regular physical activity, by maintaining a good muscle reserve, by eating a variety of foods to supply nutrients and brain fuel and by the efficient actions of the hormone insulin, which, you will recall, is also boosted by physical activity.

Hydration

Your brain cannot fire on all cylinders when you are even a little bit dehydrated no matter what your age, how much exercise you get or how much good food you eat. If dehydration worsens it can present the brain with almost insurmountable challenges, bringing on confusion and incoherence surprisingly quickly, something which becomes increasingly likely as you get older.

Without adequate hydration, neurons just can't communicate with each other, which after all is what cognition is all about. Dehydration also affects blood flow through the brain, which results in both potential reduction of available nutrients to the brain and, most significantly, a release of stress hormones. Excessive levels of these stress hormones affect production of neurotransmitters and mess up the actions of not only the neurons themselves but also the glial cells so they can't support and protect the neurons.

If you become unwell, even mild dehydration makes delirium far more likely — and that is a significant issue in itself for your brain — causing confusion, hallucination and falls especially, but also being associated with increased likelihood of developing long-term cognitive issues.

But even knowing how important hydration is, getting enough fluid is often a challenge because increasing age means you don't feel thirsty as soon as you should. That happens for a whole lot of reasons, but basically because some of the mechanisms that would usually be monitoring hydration levels and sending messages if the levels start to fall, are affected by ageing: the messages just don't get through. So feeling thirsty becomes a less and less useful measure of fluid needs as people move into their later years. As well, some messages about thirst are combined with hunger, so if appetite declines for food, with it can go the messages to drink what the body needs.

On top of all that, whenever your food intake is down, so is the amount of fluid available to body and brain. That's partly because some of the water our bodies get each day comes from the food we eat and some from the digestive process as foods are broken down. So not eating well makes dehydration even more likely.

Water is the ideal drink for younger people to keep up fluids, especially during activity. No matter what marketing might suggest, it is really only elite athletes and people doing hard physical activity in hot, dry conditions who need the additional sugars and electrolytes in 'energy' drinks. For younger people eating well, the extra sugar these drinks contain is not helpful for the body or the brain.

' Getting enough fluid is often a challenge because increasing age means you don't feel thirsty as soon as you should. '

But for older people, especially those who have a declining appetite, who are eating smaller amounts of food, or who are living with dementia, getting fluids along with nutrition is often very useful. Getting hung up on encouraging these people to drink water can actually do more harm than good: a big drink of lovingly encouraged water can 'fill them up' so eating a nutritious meal afterwards can pose quite a challenge. For the frail elderly and for those living with cognitive decline or dementia, any fluid is useful (and for some reason many people with dementia tend to dislike water) so soft drinks, cordials, sweetened tea or coffee, and flavoured milks are useful fluid sources.

There are some delicious drink recipes in this book that will give vital fluids along with useful nutrients.

Mood food?

Can specific foods boost neurotransmitters and improve moods and brain function? Neurotransmitters work throughout the brain and body and also in the digestive tract, facilitating communication between neurons and, in the digestive system, between the bacteria there. The gut bacteria make their own neurotransmitters but are also influenced by those released on instruction from the brain into the gut. Conversely, the brain makes its own, but there are also substances produced by the gut bacteria that are able to influence the brain's neurotransmitter production. Read more about the gut–brain axis in Chapter 6.

Different neurotransmitters are made from specific amino acids (building blocks of proteins) that need to be brought in across the blood–brain barrier.

We have already discussed how the blood–brain barrier acts like a security cordon to protect the highly vulnerable brain from potential unwanted intruders. It's great at that job, but unfortunately, like any security barrier, it can slow down the passage of things that you do want to get in as much as things you don't. The blood–brain barrier allows nutrients through, but in the case of amino acids, it acts a bit like a car ferry on a river crossing: safe passage is assured, but only so many vehicles can get across at any one time. There are

specific 'ferries' for amino acids, but only a certain number of them and the ferry operators don't play favourites: it's a first-in-first-served system. So even though brain cells may be waiting on the other side for specific amino acids to make specific neurotransmitters, the ones they need have to wait in line with other amino acids being ferried over for different tasks. It's not hard to see how easily that can slow down production, especially at times when the needs are high.

There have been ideas put forward, and you may have even read advice, about foods or supplements you can eat to boost certain brain chemicals (such as boosting serotonin by taking supplements or eating foods high in tryptophan to reduce depression). The idea is that, by providing the particular amino acids that are used in the manufacture of one or another neurotransmitter, you can get the brain to make more of the one you want.

But the blood–brain barrier gets in the way of that, literally and figuratively, because we eat proteins that contain all sorts of amino acids (most having no association at all with neurotransmitters) and it's only during digestion that the amino acids are released from those proteins. After that, they have to deal with the 'ferry' system, and when a meal has contained lots of different amino acids there is no guarantee that the ones needed will make it across quickly.

Some care has to be taken with attempts to manipulate brain chemistry. Eating foods reputed to be high in certain amino acids is very unlikely to do harm because no food is made entirely of one type of amino acid. But taking a supplement is more like taking a medication and might do more harm than good if it's not done under medical supervision: just because

Fat is not always the bad guy it's been thought of for years. It's a normal component of many natural foods — meats, dairy foods, nuts, seeds, oils, grains and some vegetables — and it carries many of the flavour components of foods. It gives foods a creamy mouthfeel and, importantly, is great at keeping appetite up to scratch in older people who are more likely to struggle with reduced appetite than younger adults (who most often have the opposite problem!).

The marine omega-3 fats get a lot of interest and so many people seem to take one or other type of fish- or krill-oil supplement. These contain the DHA and EPA that are found in high concentrations in the brain and have a variety of vital roles in cognitive function (as well as in other parts of the body; the heart most of all). There has been an abundance of research work done on DHA because of its especially important role in protecting brain cells; however, as already mentioned, it's not exactly clear how what you eat relates to what ends up in the brain. It's most likely that all the omega-3s have important roles to play, although medical research has not yet completely identified those roles, so relying on only one type may cause you to miss some benefits the others can provide. As discussed already, ALA may help your brain cells keep up fuel supplies, and EPA looks like it may help limit the production of *beta* amyloid.

And it is important to be aware that the large amounts you can take in when you get omega-3 from supplements is nowhere near what you can get from food, and that can have unintended consequences for some people. Omega-3 in high doses, for some people, can thin the blood so that bleeding is difficult to stop. Also, as is the case with anything you take as a supplement in large doses, they can unbalance other nutrients. When taking these in the doses contained in most fish-oil supplements, they are not acting as nutrients, but more like medications and must be considered in that way.

Omega-3s are also contributors to oxidation reactions in brain cells: that's good, but the wastes produced need to be balanced by antioxidants so that excess oxidative wastes are mopped up. If you take omega-3 supplements you need to balance them with antioxidant foods, but at very high doses it's hard to eat enough for that balance.

Always let your doctor know if you are taking any tablets, including omega-3 supplements: they may seem innocuous but they need to be considered in light of all of the above and also in line with other medications you might be taking.

Interestingly, the widely touted Mediterranean diet and the acclaimed diets of some Asian countries may well gain their plusses from the abundance of antioxidants they supply from fruit, vegetables, legumes and good-quality olive oil along with the omega-3s and good protein from fish and seafood.

Sources of omega-3

ALA: flaxseeds (linseeds), walnuts and less in other nuts; leafy green vegetables; some oils, particularly canola.

EPA and DHA (also called long-chain omega-3s): fish oil, fish and other seafood, especially oily cold-water fish such as salmon, tuna, mackerel and sardines; smaller amounts in grass-fed meats and poultry; wild meats (like kangaroo and rabbit); egg yolks; the brain and liver of meat animals; milk and dairy products from free-ranging, grass-fed cows.

something isn't made by a pharmaceutical company and prescribed by your doctor, it doesn't mean it won't act like a medication with side effects and therapeutic implications.

And then there is the added issue that the same 'ferries' that transport amino acids sometimes also have to take things other than amino acids across, thus potentially slowing, or at least complicating things further. Incidentally that includes the Parkinson's disease medication L-dopa or levodopa (brand names include *Madopar*, *Sinemet*) and this is one of the reasons it can be extra difficult to effectively treat Parkinson's disease symptoms: the medication has to compete with other amino acids from protein foods. L-dopa is a variety of the neurotransmitter dopamine.

Once the necessary amino acids do make it into the brain, they need to be manufactured into the appropriate neurotransmitter in processes that need a wide array of substances, all of which also have to make it across the barrier. Vitamins, minerals, antioxidant substances, certain fatty acids (including omega-3 oils) and fuel to run the production, are all needed for this work.

Many things have greater influence on the levels of various neurotransmitters than individual foods do, including stress, alcohol, inadequate diet, neurotoxins, both recreational and therapeutic drugs, and exercise. Among those, only exercise and a beneficial diet have positive effects; the rest, over the years, may lead to imbalances and reduced ability to supply what the brain needs in later life.

Phenols and brain-derived neurotrophic factor (BDNF)

Some antioxidant substances that are generally called phenols (but which include flavanols, flavones, anthocyanins, catechins and others) have been found to raise levels of BDNF in the blood. These substances are found in a huge variety of foods and are largely responsible for either, or both, their colour or intense flavour. You might read about the exceptional importance of individual foods such as blueberries, herbs and spices like rosemary or turmeric, coffee or extra virgin olive oil in boosting production of BDNF. All of these and hundreds more contain phenols (or phenolic compounds) and the reality is that the answer lies in mixing them up.

As discussed previously, just because BDNF levels in the blood increase at times, doesn't mean the same happens in the brain; and physical activity has a more powerful effect anyway than anything you eat.

The recipes in this book don't cover all the possible antioxidants in food, but they abound with colour to give you a good chance at getting a good variety. You can increase your antioxidant and especially your phenol intake by also including other foods listed on page 39. You don't need to eat every food every day, but mixing it up recipe by recipe, meal by meal and day by day will always be a good idea.

chapter 5

Eating for brain maintenance

The human body is a marvellous and too often underestimated system: it's able to get the resources it needs from the huge variety of foods we eat every day. If resources are not immediately available it can usually make do, for a while at least: when it comes to the brain that might mean your thinking is a bit sluggish, temporarily — and, let's face it, we all have those days — but it may not matter so much in the long term. However, if it happens repeatedly over the years, small amounts of damage to individual cells, structures and the systems that provide the brain with resources can occur, adding up and eventually contributing to the development of dementia.

As yet, we don't really know exactly what the process leading to a dementia diagnosis is, but it certainly makes sense to keep the brain well resourced with protective substances.

Many people know about *beta* amyloid (Aβ) plaques that are thought to be associated with the development of Alzheimer's disease. But what you might not know is that Aβ is a normal brain protein that somehow starts doing unusual things. One of those is to 'stick together' into plaques thought to block the sending of signals between individual nerves.

Scientists now think the 'unusual' behaviour of Aβ, and potentially other problems that occur in brain cells, might be a result of damage accumulated over many years. Once the accumulation starts, it drives more damage, creating a vicious cycle.

There are three main ways that food can help reduce that damage:
- keeping chronic inflammation at bay;
- providing antioxidants for cell protection;
- helping maintain smooth, unimpeded blood flow.

Chronic inflammation

Inflammation is actually something that is meant to happen in the body: it is part of the body's defence systems, helping us fight off illness and infection. It helps set up for and manage any repair work that's needed if damage has occurred, by employing an array of communicator chemicals to put defence systems on high alert, activating body systems and orchestrating the redirection of resources when there is an active threat to be dealt with. Problems occur because, unfortunately, too often the system doesn't switch off as it should when the threat has ceased and sometimes it starts up without a real threat having occurred. This is called chronic inflammation and it means brain and body cells are using extra resources and producing extra toxic wastes, but with the system chronically inflamed, the usual clean-up processes to deal with these wastes are not given priority. The consequence for the brain eventually is exhaustion in some areas and the build-up of substances like Aβ. Inflammation is thought by many researchers to be the biggest challenge to our health as we age for these reasons, as well as for its effects elsewhere in the body.

So why does this happen? We don't have complete answers yet, but there are many things we know play a part and that we can easily work with to increase our own chance of keeping it under control.

Inactivity and lack of regular exercise stand out as the biggest contributors in most research. Living a sedentary lifestyle is associated with a reduced brain volume, and increasing the activity levels of previously sedentary people reduces inflammatory activity. Therefore, exercise wins again, increasing the chance of maintaining good brain function.

Other research has shown that there is just too much food available to most of us living in the developed world. It's not just obesity in young or middle adulthood that is the issue here, although they certainly are of concern; but inflammation is triggered by regularly eating more food than your body needs each day (even if you don't get fat from that). Obesity drives chronic inflammation, and the combination of the two makes things worse.

Take care again to consider your stage of life when you think about this. Avoiding chronic overconsumption in younger and middle age

is where the benefits lie: it's about eating meals as needed and not giving in to the constant marketing that seems to suggest every waking moment needs to involve putting something in your mouth. No matter how *nutritious* some foods are, adding them to an already complete day's meals might do more harm than good.

When you are past middle age the best thing to do is boost your activity levels in any way you can (or keep them up if you are already doing that) because that's a sure-fire way to do your body a favour. Exercise reduces inflammation in the body and the brain.

‘ **Exercise reduces inflammation in the body and the brain.** ’

As you advance in age you need to be sure to keep up your nutrition, remembering that you need the same amount of most nutrients and more of some, including protein, so you must not let your food intake dwindle. Dieting for weight loss at later age is not a good idea, but boosting exercise and muscle activity will always be of more help in combating inflammation than anything else.

When eating to prevent inflammation, it is often the same foods that protect the body from oxidative stress that come out on top in protection against inflammation. Many of the substances you know as antioxidants (and that are listed on page 39) are also able to combat excessive inflammation. Some, including flavonoids, resveratrol and others, have antioxidant actions throughout the body but also can move across the blood–brain barrier where they have important neuroprotective and anti-inflammatory roles. Additionally, a number of foods supply substances known to reduce inflammation and protect cells: these include oily fish for its omega-3 fats; nuts, seeds and avocados for their monounsaturated fats and fibre; beans and legumes for their fibre and other important substances; and the oil from olives and nuts. With all oils, but especially olive oil, choose the ones that have undergone the fewest steps in their production: extra virgin olive oil contains antioxidants as well as protective compounds that are reduced with further refining. Always choose oils that have had as little processing as possible, and mix up the types you use to get some variety.

Cooking and processing

There are many things we do to foods before we actually eat them. Some are essential for making foods safe to eat, but there are thousands of products on supermarket shelves that have undergone varying degrees of change from their original form. Freezing, canning, drying or other forms of preservation are of little consequence, but it does look like some foods that bear little or no resemblance to their origins are a problem. Foods that are commercially processed, specifically if that involves heating or cooking at high temperatures, especially repeatedly and with the addition of extra fats, sugars, salt, flavouring or preservatives, all tend to increase inflammation. Deep-fried or baked foods that are high in salt or sugar, including many prominent takeaway (take-out) foods are possible culprits too. It seems that the further a food ends up from where it started out, the more likely it might be to contribute to chronic inflammation. The best advice is to try to eat foods that remain as close as possible to the way they came off the land, from the animal, or from the sea.

That doesn't mean you should never enter a supermarket or eat 'fast food' again: for most people they provide a convenient, accessible source of food. But add as many fresh foods as you can: vegetables, fruits, meat, fish, dairy, nuts, seeds and legumes along with good oils.

Oxidation

Oxidation is the process that each of your body cells uses to carry out its unique function. It is absolutely essential to life, but also results in waste products you might know as 'free radicals', oxidants or oxidative waste. One way cells are protected is by removing these from within and around cells to avoid harm. This is especially important in your brain, because its immense workload and capacity means that more oxidation happens there than in any other organ in your body. As we live longer, the accumulation of even tiny amounts of damage, left behind if oxidative wastes are not cleaned up, can eventually swamp your brain's abilities.

Some scientists have recently suggested that *beta* amyloid (Aβ) accumulation might start as part of the brain's attempt at self-protection in the face of oxidative stress (when oxidative damage is accumulating). But something goes wrong. Instead of Aβ providing protection and then being removed, it accumulates, forming disruptive plaques thought to eventually impact cognitive functions. It may also be that the glia are part of what goes wrong, by not being able to help remove excess Aβ when affected by inflammation and oxidative stress.

Even if research finds that Aβ is not the supreme culprit it's been thought of until recently, oxidative damage is still thought to drive many changes that impact neurons and glia. It seems that oxidative damage messes up

ANTIOXIDANT	SOURCE
ANTHOCYANINS	intensely coloured foods (including orange, pink, scarlet, purple, red and blue), especially in purple or red fruits and vegetables including berries, red grapes and red wine, plums, eggplant (aubergine) skin, cherries, red lettuce or other vegetables with red or purple colour, raw cocoa powder and dark chocolate.
CARNOSINE	meats, chicken, fish, venison, rabbit and any game meat: it's found in the muscles of animals and is higher in muscles that do a lot of exercise, so grass-fed and wild meats will have more.
CATECHINS	apples, cocoa, white and green tea.
CHOLINE	egg yolk, meats and fish, whole grains.
TURMERIC (CURCUMIN)	the dark yellow spice used commonly in many Indian, Asian and Middle Eastern dishes.
FLAVONOIDS	darker green vegetables such as kale and spinach, broccoli, parsley, cauliflower, black teas, coffee (but not instant coffee), seaweed and all sorts of soya foods, apples and citrus fruits.
LYCOPENE, CAROTENE	citrus fruits (including marmalade because quantities are high in skin and pith), yellow and orange fruits and vegetables, apples, tea, tomatoes and all tomato products, and watermelon.
LUTEIN, ZEAXANTHIN	kale, spinach and similar leafy green vegies, sweet corn, yellow and orange vegetables and fruit, egg yolks, pink-fleshed fish and seafood (including salmon and prawns).
OTHER POLYPHENOLS	coffee, green and black tea, whole grains, onions, garlic, ginger, mushrooms, flaxseed (linseed), sesame seeds, lentils.
RESVERATROL	peanuts, pistachios, red grape skins and red wine, blueberries, cocoa, dark chocolate.
SELENIUM	nuts (especially Brazil nuts), fish, seafood, liver, kidney, red meat, chicken, eggs, mushrooms, and grains. (The level of selenium in foods usually depends on how much is in the soil in which the food is grown.)
URIDINE	tomatoes, brewer's yeast, broccoli, liver, molasses and nuts.
VITAMIN A	all yellow and orange vegetables and fruits, as well as in eggs, butter, milk, cheese and liver.
VITAMIN C	citrus fruits, berries, mango, capsicum (peppers), potatoes, cabbage, spinach and Asian greens.
VITAMIN E	wheatgerm (in wholemeal and wholegrain bread and cereals), vegetable oils, nuts, eggs, seeds, fish and avocado.
ZINC	lean red meat, liver, kidney, chicken, seafood (especially oysters), milk, whole grains, legumes and nuts.

Antioxidants go by a variety of names and are categorised in many ways. This table gives an overview of commonly recognised types and the foods in which they are found.

the ability of brain cells to use glucose properly and disrupts the workings of the mitochondria, which are the cells' power suppliers. That process becomes self-perpetuating, because mitochondria that have suffered oxidative damage then produce more oxidative waste, thereby adding to oxidative stress.

There is evidence that some people might be more susceptible to oxidative stress (and maybe inflammation) than others, so their chances of developing Alzheimer's and other dementias are increased. This probably (at least partly) comes down to genetic make-up, and while our understanding of that continues to grow and will assist in solving the puzzle in time, we are not quite there yet; however, everyone can access the protection against oxidative damage that comes from myriad and easily accessible substances that act as antioxidants. The greater variety and quantity of antioxidants you eat in real foods, the better chance you give your brain (and the rest of your body).

Antioxidants and related food components, go by a mystifying assortment of chemical names and some are also vitamins and essential minerals; however, in a delightfully convenient twist of nature, different ones also happen to come from different coloured foods. So you don't really need to know much about nutrition to make sure you get plenty of antioxidants, you just need to eat a variety of coloured foods. Ideally, eat at least five or six different coloured foods at each meal; more if you can manage it.

Many intensely coloured foods are well known sources of antioxidants: think berries, cherries, red apples, egg yolks, dark green vegetables, green herbs, black olives, multicoloured lettuce, black and green tea, turmeric and other spices, the wide array of coloured fruits and vegetables, not to mention dark chocolate and red wine! But even paler foods like green and gold apples (both the flesh and the skin), nuts, fish and mushrooms are good sources. You don't need much of each different food; you just need variety.

Some foods — such as walnuts, flaxseeds (linseeds) and flaxseed oil, canola oil — also provide the plant-based omega-3 fat ALA (see page 34), adding benefits for both the heart and the brain. Again, it's not huge amounts of any one food that does the job, it's eating as many different things as you can every day and every week, and reaping the many benefits that brings.

Don't think that antioxidants are only found in plant foods. Eggs supply choline; meats, liver and seafood supply zinc, selenium and carnosine (an antioxidant only found in animal foods, incidentally) among others. It's all about variety: when you put a protein food at the centre of the meal and surround it with as many colours as possible you cover your bases.

It's really only when the variety of foods you eat dwindles that your antioxidant intake falls. Then it may be tempting to look to commercial antioxidant supplements, drinks and tablets. Advertising claims can be seductive, convincing you that the latest berry or strange-looking fruit from the high Himalayas or South America has the secret antioxidant to override all others. But the science is clear: it's the combination of many different antioxidants that gives the best protection, and getting antioxidants from foods has the advantage over supplementation (they may not work as effectively alone as they do when they are in the food they originally came from). There are other substances in the same foods that help in ways we are only just starting to understand and, no doubt, more will be known of these in the next few years.

chapter 6

Gut health

I know it might seem somewhat strange but what is inside your gastrointestinal tract (or to give it a simpler name, your gut) has a powerful influence on your mood, behaviour and the health of your brain.

' **What is in your gut has a powerful influence on your mood, behaviour and the health of your brain.** '

There are an almost unimaginable one hundred trillion or so — that's 10^{14} for the maths buffs among you — bacteria living in the gut: so many that they are now thought of as another body organ, the gut microbiome. These many and varied bacteria are indispensable to us because they are able to harvest energy and nutrients that are otherwise unavailable from the food we eat via our own digestive systems. Some nutrients, derived from microbial breakdown of dietary fibre, are of paramount importance to the health of the gut wall itself; however, it's the array of chemical messengers they produce that are able to communicate with and influence the brain which are of most interest here.

These chemical messengers work in a number of ways: some impact the body hormone system and can influence appetite, mood, emotions and reactions to stress; some impact the production of neurotransmitters, including serotonin and *gamma*-Aminobutyric acid (GABA) — both associated more with positive emotions and calmness than stress and aggression; and it's recently been found that some also promote brain health by nurturing the glia, those cells which support and protect brain neurons. What's really interesting is that when the variety of different types of bacteria in the gut is lower (that is, when microbial diversity is reduced) the production of substances called cytokines seems to increase, and they can contribute to inflammation and thus cognitive decline and frailty.

'Good' versus 'bad'

You will have heard discussion of 'good' versus 'bad' bacteria in the gut and it is quite true that the overall health of the gut microbiome aligns with the types and diversity of bacteria that live there, with the balance of 'good' with 'bad'. When the variety of bacteria in the gut is reduced, that seems to mean it's mostly the 'good' ones that are missing; therefore, increasing diversity in the types of gut bacteria means encouraging more 'good' guys.

What's also become clear in recent years is that the health of the brain and the health of the gut microbiome are inextricably linked through what has become known as the gut–brain axis. This is effectively a communication hub, sorting information coming in from both gut and brain so that the brain is able to influence the gut, and the gut is able to influence the brain.

The brain affects the survival of different bacteria by changing things like the 'leakiness' of the gut wall (allowing some substances into the blood, while others are excluded) and its motility (the rate of pulsing that moves the contents along the gut), as well as releasing chemical messengers that create a local gut environment that helps some types of bacteria to thrive and others to decline. A number of things, including a calm outlook and good stress-management strategies, seem to swing that balance towards the 'good' guys, while anxiety and elevated stress levels give the not-so-good guys a better chance. We can influence this balance by what we eat, but, because our brain has such an important role to play, anything we can do to manage stress is essential as well.

If the balance in the microbiome is in favour of the good guys the messages going back to the brain tend to continue to be helpful, promoting better mood, reduced anxiety and reduced inflammation and, as a result, better brain health.

Social isolation seems to be related to changes in gut bacteria also: spending time with others and having a good chat, especially with a few laughs thrown in, helps keep you well. It might be a little surprising to know we share more than those laughs: we also benefit from sharing our microorganisms around, especially among members of our family.

A less-than-healthy gut microbiome can impact neurotransmitters too: a greater proportion of 'bad' bacteria, or a less-diverse microbiome, can reduce the production of the neurotransmitters GABA and serotonin in the gut. By contrast, substances produced in a healthy gut — from fibrous vegetables, nuts, pulses and grains — can boost production.

Brain influence on the gut

The vagus nerve travels between the brain and the gut and is involved in diverse processes including swallowing, digestion, heart rate, memory and feelings of stress or anxiety. When you are calm and relaxed, the vagus nerve is stimulated, resulting in a settled digestive process, calmed heart rate, improved memory and immune function, and better sleep, as well as further reducing anxiety levels. At the same time, it seems to encourage greater diversity in the gut microbiome, boost the growth of helpful bacteria and reduces chronic inflammation. In turn, those 'good' or more helpful bacteria produce substances that also stimulate the vagus nerve.

By contrast, feelings of anxiety are more likely to cause the opposite effects, with heart palpitations and gastrointestinal distress becoming more common, as well as increased inflammation, overstimulated immune response and a less healthy environment in the gut so that 'good' bacteria are discouraged.

Another big benefit of a healthy gut microbiome is that it may play a role in neuroplasticity by increasing levels of brain-derived neurotrophic factor (BDNF) in the gut and blood.

PREbiotics	
GRAINS	wholegrain wheat, oats, barley and rye and foods made from them including bread, crackers, pasta, gnocchi, couscous, quinoa, chia and various 'ancient' grains that are now more common on grocery store shelves.
VEGETABLES	chicory (this is the root of the plant, the leaves of which are often called witlof and appear in salads, although the leaves are not high in prebiotics), garlic, onion, leek, spring onions (scallions), shallots, asparagus, beetroot (beet), fennel bulb, green peas, snow peas (mangetout), sweetcorn, savoy cabbage, Jerusalem artichokes.
LEGUMES	kidney beans, lentils, chickpeas (garbanzo beans), all dried beans.
FRUITS	white peaches, nectarines, watermelon, persimmon, custard apples, tamarillos, grapefruit, pomegranate seeds, dried fruit (especially dates and figs), green or under-ripe bananas (not ripe bananas).
NUTS AND SEEDS	pistachios, cashews.

PRObiotics	
COMMERCIAL PREPARATIONS	tablets or powders as discussed in this chapter.
FERMENTED FOODS NOTE: contrary to some advice on the internet, most cheese is not fermented unless it's labelled that way. * these foods are both pre- and pro-biotic	• yoghurt containing live bacteria (from any type of milk: cow, sheep, goat or alternatives) • cheese made from unpasteurised milk (sale of such cheeses is allowed in Australia now, as long as manufacturers follow strict guidelines for looking after their dairy cows and producing the cheese. These cheeses are generally produced by small, artisan cheesemakers), 'blue' or blue-veined cheeses, made using bacterial spores to form the blue, grey or creamy coloured mould giving them their characteristic look, flavour and aroma • lassi (fermented milk drink) and other fermented drinks such as kombucha • kimchi*; sauerkraut*; and naturally fermented pickles*: you need to look for labels that indicate the presence of probiotic or beneficial bacteria, or make them yourself. Many commercial 'pickles' are made using vinegar and are heated; they taste great and are a means of preserving vegetables and fruits for eating out of season, but these varieties don't generally contain useful, live bacteria. • naturally fermented apple cider and other fruit vinegars also often contain beneficial bacteria. • tempeh* (fermented soybean curd) and miso • good-quality or homemade sourdough bread made using a slow, traditional fermentation process (it will be chewy and have the traditional sour taste if it's fermented)

You are not expected to change your personality, but finding a way to manage anxiety is well worth the effort to help your gut as well as your brain. Activity, exercise, social interaction, laughter and avoiding an overly sedentary lifestyle are powerful. Depression and mental illness seem to be associated with a less-than-healthy gut microbiome and vice versa, and this in turn may have something to do with cognitive decline. So, if you are living with depression or anxiety then medication, psychological therapy, meditation, yoga, acupuncture or whatever works for you to help you manage the problem will probably also help your brain health in the long term. And improving your diet and lifestyle along the lines suggested in this book will be of great assistance to both gut and brain.

Food for a healthy gut microbiome

When it comes to food you can do a lot to boost 'good' bacteria:

- encourage the growth of good bacteria already in the gut by providing nutrients they particularly like, from '*pre*biotic' foods. These are fibrous foods such as pulses, beans, nuts, seeds, cabbage, onions and root vegetables.
- introduce new good bacteria by taking '*pro*biotics' or eating foods that contain beneficial bacteria. These include probiotic capsules, drinks or powders (it is probably best to buy refrigerated products, as they contain live bacteria, but there will be more shelf-stable probiotic powders that supply bacteria in spore form entering the market), and fermented foods in the list opposite.
- minimise foods that are thought to swing the balance of bacteria towards the 'bad' guys:

these tend to be foods that have undergone more processing and contain high amounts of cooking fats, salt, flavour additives and added sugars (think battered and fried foods, commercial biscuits/cookies, commercial cakes, pastries and desserts, most so-called 'fast foods', snack foods like chips and similar, soft drinks and confectionery).

The thing about both pre- and pro-biotics is they really can't do harm and often provide all sorts of other useful nutrients as well, so they are definitely worth a try. But take care if you don't usually eat a lot of prebiotic foods, because the fibre and other substances in them can create lots of wind! If you want to eat more of them, or start adding new things, do so gradually and build up the amount to give the bacteria in your gut a chance to get used to the change, to adapt and for the right sorts of bacteria to gradually increase and help your digestion.

If you already have issues with bloating and abdominal pain then get advice before adding prebiotics to your diet because they are likely to make those things worse.

There are many other strategies being developed and a lot of research going on right now to find the best way to achieve a healthy gut microbiome beyond using pre- and pro-biotics. That is likely to be different for different people and might even involve a scary concept known as a faecal transplant, which is a procedure in which gut bacteria are removed from a healthy gut, or those from a less-healthy gut are 'cleaned' to end up with a higher number of 'good' bacteria; the bacteria are then reintroduced to the gut to swing the balance there towards the good. As they say, 'watch this space': this is definitely something you will hear a lot about in the next few years and beyond.

chapter 7

Obesity and diabetes

What does your weight have to do with your brain health?

As mentioned in Chapter 5, being overweight or obese in early and middle adulthood contributes to chronic inflammation and therefore is not good for your brain. Anything you can do to lose excess weight in those years is essential; and any way you can avoid being sedentary, boost your activity levels and get good muscle activity into your daily regime is a powerful brain protector.

❛ **Weight loss in later years causes loss of body muscle, which is likely to do more harm than good.** ❜

But the thinking around changing your eating habits when you are in your 70s and beyond needs to be different. The advice about staying active and getting good exercise doesn't change, but dieting to lose weight is no longer the best plan. It's not that obesity is a good thing, it's more that weight loss in those later years causes loss of body muscle, which is likely to do more harm than good, so the advice should not be the same. That might sound strange in this day and age, but it's essential that those who are in their senior years understand the distinction for the sake of their bodies *and* their brains.

This is an interesting area to look at because 'ideal' body weight also changes as you age. As long as it is underpinned with physical activity and maintaining muscle, it may be that a bit of extra body fat in these later years actually protects your brain. By that I mean the bit of extra padding we might, in years gone by, have called 'middle-aged spread'. The statistics certainly support this: when whole populations of 70-year-olds are looked at, people who would have been at the higher end of the weight scales — even considered overweight — in their 40s or 50s, experience less illness and are more likely to be alive 10 years on, than those who were at the low end of the weight scales.

Of course, this is not true for every individual person, and there are plenty of fit, well-muscled, lean 70-year-olds who will live to a healthy 90 years or so, but overall a slightly heavier weight for active older people is no longer considered to be a bad thing and may, in fact, be helpful.

This could be related to the tiny amounts of some hormones produced by body fat, which are able to exert positive influence on brain function: this supply is pretty much irrelevant when you are younger, as it is swamped by what your body is producing elsewhere, but in your later years, when production in the rest of the body has all but ceased, it looks like this otherwise insignificant hormone supply from body fat can give the brain some help.

Another consideration is that people who are a bit heavier are probably eating more food and the extra nutrients are bound to be doing good! Whatever the reason, it's worth reassessing your ideal weight as the years move on.

Fasting and the brain

There's been lots of discussion in recent years of the benefits to your body (and, more recently, your brain) of eating fewer kilojoules (calories) than you might feel you need during adulthood (usually called kilojoule/calorie restriction), or the health rewards from intermittent fasting (periods of time when you don't eat at all, or eat an extremely limited diet).

There is good reason for this: practising some sort of kilojoule restriction — that is, short periods of little or no food intake without necessarily causing weight loss — when you are a young adult, or in middle adulthood, may well assist with cognition later in life, mainly by reducing the inflammation and oxidative stress caused by over-nutrition.

‘ Taking up kilojoule restriction when you are already over 65 needs very careful weighing up of the risks versus the possible benefits. ’

In addition it seems that long-term kilojoule restriction might be able to help brain cells use ketones to assist in fuel supply when glucose use is low. But these practices need to be started early in life and must be combined with good activity levels to help maintain muscle as devotees move into later life. Taking up kilojoule restriction when you are already over 65 needs very careful weighing up of the risks versus the possible benefits.

What's interesting is that many people now living well in their 80s and beyond in fact probably had some sort of kilojoule restriction in their younger lives, whether that was because of a childhood in which food was just not as plentiful as it is now, or during wartime and food rationing. It wasn't called by a fancy name; it was just life, but it might have incidentally given the benefit so many now strive for.

For people who are now 70 or more years old, kilojoule-restricted eating plans can only safely be carried out by combining a highly nutritious, protein- and nutrient-dense diet that also restricts energy (requiring a very good understanding of nutrition) with the following provisos:

- it must include a well-planned exercise schedule to avert muscle loss and preferably also avoid weight loss.
- weight loss should *not* be the aim: weight maintenance is essential, even if you consider yourself overweight, because of the possible damage that losing body muscle could do outweighing potential cognitive benefits.

The really good news from the research is that exercise does the same sorts of things for your brain that periods of reduced food also do, so the importance of getting the exercise recommended throughout this book cannot be overstated.

There are definite advantages for your brain, it seems, from not only keeping your body weight down to a good healthy level during most of your adulthood, but also from eating just a bit less than what is on offer.

No matter what your age, the most important thing anyone can do is to get plenty of exercise of all types and keep your body moving: this gives you the muscle reserve you need for later life as well as the other benefits exercise provides the brain. For anyone who is considered 'overweight' and just can't manage to achieve the result on the scales no matter what you do, every effort to stay physically active, flexible and fit will do your brain good.

For young adults and people up to perhaps their late 60s, tackling overweight as soon as possible in whatever way works for you is important. If that requires a weight-loss

'No matter what your age, the most important thing anyone can do is to get plenty of exercise of all types and keep your body moving.'

diet, periods of intermittent fasting or just sometimes embracing the concept of feeling hungry for a few extra hours, that can be very helpful. It does much more than just making it easier to move around: it reduces inflammation and holds off insulin resistance, among so many more effects that help your brain health.

But if you are beyond your late 60s, the situation with body weight is different. Certainly, if carrying the excess is stopping you getting about and being able to do some activities you would like to, or making life harder for your joints, it would seem ideal to shed some of the excess if possible; however, unless you can achieve that along with an extremely good muscle exercise program, you will lose muscle in the process — in larger amounts than would happen in younger people — and that, as you have read, is not helpful for your body or your brain. In fact, the increased likelihood of poor wound healing, slower recovery from illness, accident or surgery, insulin resistance, increased likelihood of falls, potential issues with brain-fuel supply and a number of other factors potentially carry worse consequences than a bit of extra body weight.

In these years, if you can get involved in a program that mixes very good exercise — particularly resistance exercise (anything that makes your muscles work against a resistance, such as using gym weight machines, carrying the shopping, digging and gardening, walking upstairs, swimming or doing water activities using underwater dumbbells, or cycling up an incline) — with a well-designed higher-protein diet so that you are maintaining muscle while losing fat, that is great!

Unintentional weight loss

If, like many of us, you have spent years of your life struggling to keep your weight down, working hard to ignore enticing treats and dreading what the scales will tell you, then finding that a time comes along in your later life when the weight can fall off without much effort can seem like a gift that's been a long time coming! I'm sorry to say, it's far from that.

Unintentional weight loss is not a sign of health when you are in your late 60s and beyond. Not only does it signal potentially damaging muscle loss, but since close to half the people who are diagnosed with dementia

' Unintentional weight loss is not a sign of health when you are in your late 60s and beyond. '

are found to have lost weight in the year prior, it can signal problems with your brain too. That doesn't mean that all unintentional weight loss puts you on a path to dementia: far from it. Weight loss is very common if a spouse, family member or a good friend dies, as well as in times of stress and, of course, due to illness or accident. What it does mean is that you need to do all you can to maintain weight, stay active and to regain any weight lost if you can. If you do lose weight without intending to, discuss it with your doctor and get things checked out: there may be an issue you can fix, and that will help you maintain your body as well as your brain for many more years.

Diabetes

Research shows that the chances of developing dementia are higher in people who have diabetes. That doesn't mean it is inevitable by any stretch, but it does mean that it's important to look at what could be at play in diabetes, or in insulin resistance (often a forerunner to type 2 diabetes), that might impact your brain and how you can help.

You will recall from Chapter 4 that the smooth running and therefore the health of the brain relies on a constant supply of glucose from the blood because it neither makes nor stores it itself. That supply is dependent on the hormone insulin. Insulin moves glucose out of the blood into the cells where it can be used; if it is absent, or not working as it should, the levels of glucose rise in the blood, while the cells miss out.

People with type 1 diabetes produce no insulin at all, while people with type 2 either don't make enough, or what they make is not as effective as it should be. Insulin resistance can be part of type 2 diabetes, or a condition in itself: cells become unable to 'recognise' insulin as they should, and one result is the body producing more insulin to get the excess glucose out of the blood, so you can end up with excessive levels of both insulin and glucose in the blood.

It's well recognised that both excessive and very low levels of glucose in the blood are damaging, and medical management of diabetes aims to keep blood glucose levels as close as possible to what someone without diabetes would experience. Research suggests that it's mostly high blood glucose levels, happening over many years, that might contribute to the link between diabetes and various health issues including heart and

kidney disease. When it comes to diabetes and dementia, that's part of the picture also.

But what has become apparent more recently is that excessive levels of insulin, as occur in insulin resistance and often type 2 diabetes, also impact the brain.

Before we move on, while there are somewhat different considerations in managing diabetes, depending on which type you have, all have one thing in common: physical activity and maintaining a good muscle reserve is more important than anything else. A physically active 50-year-old with diabetes has a better chance at good brain health in the decades to come than his or her sedentary, overweight friend without diabetes.

When it comes to managing glucose in diabetes, both too much in the blood (*hyper*glycaemia) and too little (*hypo*glycaemia), can cause problems for the brain.

In hypoglycaemia, which really only happens in people who need to inject insulin or who take certain medications that boost body insulin production (in type 1 diabetes or some with type 2), glucose levels fall so low that brain cells cannot function and the results include extreme confusion and incoordination (not a fashion faux pas, but a medical term that signifies a lack of coordination of body movements) and eventually can cause loss of consciousness. In later age, severe hypoglycaemia can cause brain-cell death.

But the effects on the brain of milder hypoglycaemia can be different depending on your age: when you are young it seems that repeated episodes of mild hypoglycaemia that don't progress to confusion or incoordination (these tend to occur occasionally when blood glucose control is 'tight' — that is, kept within a very restricted range — the pinnacle of

medical management of diabetes for young people) may actually induce some sort of adaptation by brain cells that is beneficial to cognition. That's great, because long-term diabetes management guidelines for younger adults advocate this 'tight' control.

By contrast, when you have had diabetes for a long time, or it's been diagnosed in later years and you are now in your 70s or beyond, repeated episodes of hypoglycaemia, which of course means repeated episodes of undersupply of fuel to brain cells, is more likely to be unhelpful to the brain, eventually reducing cognition and possibly contributing to dementia. Unfortunately more severe hypoglycaemia can become more common with age, because at later age it comes on more quickly and the ability to recognise the usual warning signs can be reduced.

Things are also different when it comes to hyperglycaemia. It might seem that an excess of glucose circulating in the blood could supply extra fuel for brain activity and therefore boost cognition; however, sadly, it's quite the opposite.

Blood glucose levels that stay above normal increase the production of oxidative wastes, they also increase inflammation, cause the accumulation of toxic advanced glycation end products (AGEs) and upset the fine balance in a number of important systems in the brain.

AGEs are a combination of glucose with other things such as proteins: each component is effectively harmless individually, but when combined into AGEs, become toxic to brain and other cells. Minimising the harm AGEs can cause depends on a combination of reducing the amounts made and removing any formed from the brain, before they get the chance to do harm. AGEs are produced everywhere in the body, in every one of us as we age, but diabetes both increases the likelihood of their production and reduces the ability of the brain to clear them away. AGEs themselves also increase oxidative stress and contribute to the accumulation of *beta* amyloid (Aβ) and other damaging substances.

The good news is that the same things that fight damaging oxidation and protect all body cells, including the brain, antioxidants, also help reduce AGE production and accumulation inside the body. The antioxidants in berries and coloured vegetables, vitamins C and B6, and some minerals including selenium and zinc are especially beneficial.

' The brain thrives when glucose levels in the blood are as constant and predictable as possible. '

I should mention that not only are AGEs produced inside the body, but they can also come from some cooked or processed foods, creating problems especially if these are eaten in excess. Having foods high in sugar, such as soft drinks and confectionery, and eating processed snack foods, especially those high in sugar as more than an occasional treat, increases the chances that they can cause harm. Also, AGEs are formed when high-protein foods such as meats are cooked hot and dry, as happens on a barbecue, or when meat is heavily browned in cooking. Slower, moist cooking of meat; the use of acids such as lemon juice or vinegar in cooking; and not choosing 'well done' meat all the time all reduce the amount you might eat. Again, balance in eating is essential: meats offer valuable protein and other nutrients, so always eating them with plenty of

different antioxidant-rich coloured vegetables and fruits counters possible harm.

Staying on the straight and narrow

Not only do both high and low blood glucose levels themselves present problems, but the brain thrives when glucose levels in the blood are as constant and predictable as possible, not swinging between too high and too low. In people without diabetes, insulin is able to automatically react to small changes in blood glucose levels, so they achieve the constancy the brain enjoys — always staying within a fairly tight range without ever going too high or too low.

For those with diabetes it seems that, not only does the brain benefit from good blood glucose control achieving that same constancy, but when blood glucose levels fluctuate a lot with bigger highs and smaller lows during the day occurring regularly, that is another trigger for damaging inflammation.

Elevated insulin levels

In people with insulin resistance and in most people with type 2 diabetes, blood insulin levels will be higher than normal. As well, a number of substances associated with insulin — including insulin-like growth factor (IGF) and many others — behave differently when this happens.

Insulin has some extra and vital roles in the brain unrelated to its association with glucose: it assists with learning and the formation of memories and helps regulate a number of neurotransmitters. As well, along with some of its associated substances, it assists in neuroplasticity and other cognitive functions; however, to do any of those things it's needed in just the right amount.

If brain insulin levels are too low, then so may be some neurotransmitters, there is likely to be a struggle to learn and form new memories and the brain's ability to adapt to localised damage through neuroplasticity will be reduced. But when blood insulin levels are higher than 'just right', there are a number of longer-term consequences that can reduce brain health. One of those is that high insulin levels increase inflammation, with its toxic consequences.

Insulin — like all substances in the brain whether vital to its function or merely waste products — needs to be removed to maintain those 'just right' levels. The systems that break down insulin and remove it from the brain also happen to be involved with the removal of *beta* amyloid (Aβ), and here's where problems occur: insulin gets preferential treatment over Aβ, so if insulin levels are high, removal of Aβ slows down and the chance of amyloid plaque forming increases.

As well, changes in the way many of insulin's associates work increase the chance that other changes in the brain associated with dementia (the tangling of a protein called 'tau' that disrupts nerve transmission, for example) will develop. If blood glucose levels are high as well (as can occur in type 2 diabetes if it is not managed well) there is a double effect.

You can clearly see the problem elevated insulin levels pose for the brain, but — at the risk of being accused of sounding like a broken record — maintaining a good muscle reserve and keeping muscles working with activity and exercise will always help, mostly by reducing insulin resistance and thus insulin levels in the body.

Abdominal fat and insulin resistance

The majority of people who are carrying excessive amounts of body fat around their abdomen, especially in early or middle adulthood, are also likely to be insulin resistant, whether they know it or not.

Unfortunately, when insulin resistance and excess body fat combine it amplifies the problems described above. This abdominal accumulation is, in part, a result of insulin resistance and while we know it's not always helpful, especially in middle age, it's not always such a problem in later age because some degree of increase in waistline might be inevitable in those years.

This might be as a result of small alterations in height due to compression in the spinal column (not the sort that causes pain or structural problems, just the result of decades of the effects of gravity and the degradation of discs between vertebrae) and reduced strength in abdominal muscles that might otherwise hold that belly in. Again, exercise, activity and muscle work are all the best ways to keep both insulin resistance and excess abdominal fat accumulation at bay.

chapter 8

Diet plans in the news

There is an almost endless number of different diets and, more recently, a plethora of brain-health foods, supplements and eating plans have made the pages of newspapers, magazines and online search engines. Some may help, but most are inadequate at best.

I can't analyse them all, but here are a few thoughts on what to look for that is most likely to help, and not hinder, your brain health.

Anti-inflammatory eating

What you do to food in getting it 'from paddock to plate' has the potential to create problems for your brain.

I don't love the term 'processed' when talking about food: after all, peeling and chopping a carrot is processing, but everything you do to something that ends up being a food makes a change. Sometimes those changes are necessary to allow foods to be transported to where they are eaten or to make them safe to eat: after all, not everyone has the good fortune to be able to eat food from their own farm, or to be able to go fishing every week in pristine waterways. And every food can carry substances such as bacteria, some of which can cause food poisoning if the food is not treated appropriately.

Peeling a carrot might remove a few nutrients in and under the skin, but it doesn't actually matter much because there are plenty more nutrients in a carrot; however, with some foods it does matter. Remove the outer layers of a grain of wheat and you lose some oils and fibre that have their own unique benefits.

There are also foods that must be processed so we can eat them safely: for example, soaking maize corn, a nutritionally vital food in traditional South American cuisine, in a lime solution (not lime juice from limes, but an alkaline solution similar to garden lime) is essential to form the cornmeal into dough as well as making the B vitamin, niacin, the protein and some minerals, including calcium, nutritionally available. And most meats, fish and chicken need cooking, an everyday form of food processing, to be safe to eat.

There are plenty of examples of essential and unproblematic processing of foods, but there is also an ever-increasing number of foods that bear little or no resemblance at all to their original source, and they give a completely different picture. Think extruded snack foods (crunchy spirals, flattened shapes or twists flavoured with a variety of powders or sprinkles that may have started out with great ingredients such as soya or wholegrains, but are ultimately the products of a factory, rather than the original paddock) or spreadable forms of things that don't usually spread well, vegetarian 'bacon', chicken nuggets, sports or soft drinks. Every step that a grain of wheat, a soya bean, an oilseed or a piece of chicken must undergo to become a cheesy ring, crunchy spiral, smooth spread or crispy morsel, and every extra manufactured ingredient added to the original food, might just change the way the nutrients it originally contained work in our bodies.

The more steps a food undergoes before we eat it, the more opportunities to introduce changes in the nutrients or other components it contains, resulting in the production of substances that could be harmful in the body. For example, apart from things like rolled oats, we don't generally eat milled grain: instead we eat bread or other baked goods that have incorporated additional ingredients and undergone more steps in production, often including repeated heating and cooling, which is thought to be a particular problem in some foods. It's not necessary to completely avoid everyday foods that supply all manner of vital nutrients; however, choosing those that have the fewest steps in their production and eating foods along with them that have undergone minimal steps — fruits, vegetables, nuts and cold-pressed oils — is ideal for brain health.

Certainly, as discussed in Chapter 5, some changes that happen during the processing of foods may contribute to chronic inflammation.

I always advise mostly eating foods that remain as close as possible to the way they started out. The recipes in this book offer plenty of choices: seasonal food has the advantage because you can embrace what farms have to offer day to day, although minimal processing in freezing, canning and drying can add to the variety available at different times of the year.

Mediterranean diet

The Mediterranean diet is often recognised as being important to health and it has some characteristics in common with diets in other places where people have exceptionally long life expectancy and lower rates of dementia. Such diets usually rely on lots of seasonal vegetables and, depending on what is available locally, a variety of fruits, grains, nuts and seeds, local seafoods and meats. The Mediterranean people have also traditionally eaten a lot of olive oil and this is often suggested as the 'secret ingredient' in those diets.

But published dementia rates in Italy, Greece and Spain are not especially low, despite this. In fact, in southern Europe the rates of dementia are higher than most Scandinavian countries where olive oil use is mostly low; and higher than in Japan, for example, where olive oil use can be almost nonexistent.

I need to stress here that basing health advice on reported dementia rates is not always as clear-cut as it may seem. That's because these statistics rely on people having been diagnosed reliably, and that is certainly not happening consistently worldwide: the numbers of people living with dementia might be higher in some places than is reported, just because no-one has labelled it as dementia.

The big-ticket items in the Mediterranean diet are fresh, seasonal vegetables, pulses, fruits, nuts and olives (which are, of course, a fruit), but what is too often overlooked when the focus is on the Mediterranean 'diet' or 'eating plan' is that these people were traditionally very active: they were farmers and fishers, living high-activity lives every day in communities where social interaction was part of everyday life. As is always the case, there is more to this picture than food alone.

> **6 Protein is always essential for body and brain, but its relative importance increases as we age. 9**

One important thing to mention in the context of maintaining an age-appropriate protein intake (especially making sure you get enough into later age) is that it's commonly said of the Mediterranean diet that one should avoid red meats and dairy foods and eat significant amounts of fish and seafood. Certainly, it is generally true that the traditional diets of the fishermen and rural dwellers in the Mediterranean contained plenty of seafood and not as much red meat, but the same can't necessarily be said of the people living around the Mediterranean today and there are many examples of populations living a long way from the ocean, without ready access to fresh seafood, who do not necessarily have poor brain health.

The locally sourced fish and wild meats that traditional Mediterranean dwellers would have eaten no doubt provided brain benefits, and they would have been balanced by the vegetables and other staples of the diet as mentioned above. The meats (and dairy foods) eaten traditionally were usually from pasture-raised goats or sheep, with occasional wild meats such as rabbit.

Interestingly, much of the fish eaten in the Mediterranean region, and up into coastal countries in northern Europe, is either oily fish (usually from colder waters) or those that can be eaten whole. For people not living in areas with easy access to such fish, tinned varieties are often used.

The sort of eating in Mediterranean diet plans is exactly what is advocated in this book and generally by dietitians worldwide: your blood vessels, your heart and your brain benefit from plenty of vegetables, pulses, fruits, nuts, grains and good oils, and from food that is seasonal, has undergone minimal change or it is as close as possible to the form it started out.

When it comes to the protein foods in Mediterranean-style plans — meats, seafood, dairy, nuts, seeds and pulses — the amount best included depends on your age and stage of life, as discussed in Chapter 9. Your choice of animal or plant-based protein may well depend on factors other than nutrition: protein is always essential for body and brain, but its relative importance increases as we age. As well, I believe it's a worthwhile contribution to our societies and agricultural communities that wherever possible, we try to eat foods locally sourced and locally produced, thus reducing the costs that need to be added for transport, and reducing the impact any post-harvest inputs to those foods might have on our brains.

Turmeric, rosemary and other herbs and spices

In recent years a lot of research has been done on some herbs and spices including cinnamon, rosemary, sage and turmeric (also called curcumin). All of these are great sources of antioxidants, but there is also

quite a lot of promise in findings of their anti-inflammatory qualities.

The beautiful golden spice turmeric or curcumin — best known in dishes from India, Pakistan, Morocco and the Middle East — has created a stir in neuroscience research, being widely investigated for its anti-inflammatory actions in a number of clinical research trials. It may eventually be used in treatment of cognitive decline, but the amounts that are being tested, like many more substances that have been sourced from foods, are well beyond the amounts you would usually eat. Their actions, when eaten in tablet form, are more pharmaceutical than nutritional; however, some certainly demonstrate promise as being useful ingredients that may help brain health.

Spices of all sorts add a wide range of beneficial antioxidants, offer anti-inflammatory bonuses and taste fabulous, so are always worth adding to meals and recipes.

The quantities in the recipes in this book, and in most foods you might eat, are generally not high enough to have negative impacts. But do remember that, if you start adding tablespoons of turmeric or cinnamon to every meal, you might stray into 'pharmaceutical' territory. Anything you eat in very large amounts — even if it is a seemingly innocuous, if tasty, spice — can have anti-inflammatory or other effects potentially impacting various medications and some medical conditions, so you need to discuss any such choices with your doctor or pharmacist.

Herbs are very useful additions to foods because they can easily be grown in a small patch of garden and used in any dish to boost antioxidants and help the brain.

SUGAR AND SWEET THINGS

Our modern overprocessed diets contain so many foods high in sugar, people are right to worry about getting too much. Sugar can certainly be a problem to body and brain when it is so easy to eat excess in these foods. One thing that I say throughout this book is that, for the sake of your brain, foods need to be eaten in the form closest to the way they came from the ground, the water, plant or animal. If you do that, you avoid a lot of foods that so often contain added sugar, salt and other ingredients not in the original food. Everyday eating of these types of foods, or having sugared drinks as more than a *very* occasional treat in your life, is not brain healthy.

However, I don't consider sugar — when eaten occasionally as part of a recipe — to be a problem for most people. In these recipes, it is balanced by ingredients that boost brain health. Let's face it: desserts, cakes and ice cream are treat foods — they should not be eaten at every meal, or indulged in every day.

You can choose not to sample the sweet recipes in the Fruit and Sweet Things chapter of this book, but that frisson of delight they provide (perhaps as much as the nutrients in the nuts, spices, protein and more that they contain) is also good for your brain!

These recipes can also be used as antioxidant-rich, fibre-boosted and higher-protein extras for those for whom the lure of a sweeter treat might be the way to encourage eating and help avoid or treat the medical condition of frailty, associated with damaging weight loss and cognitive decline.

Relish away!

chapter 9

Brain health through the ages

Naturally there is more to what you eat than just the delicious recipes in this book. Here you will find meals and snacks, not whole eating plans. It's what you eat during the rest of your day that makes up your whole diet, and it is that combination that ensures you the best chance at peak brain health.

Everything in this book is underpinned by maintaining physical activity all the way through life: that's a far more powerful brain-health support than any food. As well, avoiding obesity and doing all you can to reduce excess bodyweight in youth and middle age is essential. But in later age, when maintaining muscle mass is absolutely vital and weight-loss diets cause muscle to be lost, avoiding unintentional loss or loss through dieting is more important.

How the rest of your food intake should balance these recipes depends to some extent on your age, because nutrition needs to change as the years progress, especially, as you have read in Chapter 4, when it comes to protein needs and bodyweight. Despite this, most health messages target the wider adult population and are mostly focused on people who are 30, 40 or 50.

The differences in the nutritional needs of older and younger adults, when it comes to brain health, underlie all discussions on maximising brain capacity. The brain needs the body to carry it around and to supply it with resources, and the maintenance of muscle underpins independence and physical as well as mental capacity as people get older.

If you are younger than 50

Most people who are around 40 now can expect to have another 40 or more years ahead. Their grandparents at 40, on the other hand, often could only hope for around 25 or 30 more years. That's up to an extra couple of decades that today's young adults will have, to holiday, travel and hang out with the grandkids, but it's also extra time in which tiny amounts of damage in the brain could get the chance to accumulate.

The brain has lots of great defences and mechanisms to minimise damage to its cells: if we were only expected to live to 70 as those grandparents were, any changes in cognition resulting from 'mishaps' and tiny bits of damage in the brain, might end up being insignificant in that time. But with the extra 10 to 20 or more years you can now expect beyond 70, you must be diligent about protecting your brain now.

It's important too, to be aware that the efficiency of the body's defence systems does reduce as the years advance and therefore the ability of an 80-year-old brain to protect itself is less than that of a 50-year-old.

It is never too early to eat foods that will help protect your brain in your later years. As well, this is the time to look at the overall balance of life. Every bit of physical activity you can do, everything you learn and all the ways you give your brain a chance to take a break through meditative, quiet practice and downtime, help your brain. They help build its reserves, keep chronic inflammation down and improve the efficiency of its defence and maintenance systems, all of which give it the best possible chance to maintain peak health.

This is also the time when you need to be thinking about doing everything you can to keep your weight down and maintain physical activity. Obesity in early and middle adulthood is well accepted now to be strongly predictive of later-life dementia, so everything you can do to reduce weight will be good, no matter the method you choose to lose any excess. This is also the time that intermittent fasting strategies come to the fore while you are still young enough to avoid later-life problems with unhelpful muscle loss. These fasting plans trigger responses in the body that are anti-inflammatory and therefore of great benefit to the brain.

The other very important thing to remember is that merely eating more energy in food than your body needs to use up each day, drives inflammation. So even if you are not putting on weight, if you find that you never feel 'hungry' and always leave a meal feeling just a bit stuffed full of food, it is worth thinking about skipping a meal here or there, or reducing the size of your plates so you eat just a little less.

This is certainly the time of life to focus on vegetables, salads and fruits. Your plate or bowl should contain at least half or more of these nutritious foods. Add to that grains, nuts, seeds, pulses, fish, good oils, dairy foods and meats: Mediterranean– or Asian–style diets are good. You need protein, calcium and all the nutrients in the latter group of foods, but the vegetables will give you not only the majority of the antioxidants your brain so desperately needs, but mean your meals will not tend to contain excessive kilojoules (calories). Most people at this time of life easily eat enough food to be able to pack all the nutrients needed into their day.

50 to late 60s

Everything said for the under-50s applies to this age group as well, and in these years you still have time to get rid of excess weight without muscle-loss issues, as long as you stay active.

In these years especially I want to stress the importance of avoiding too much sitting time. This applies to people who are younger too, but it's something that can become a dangerous habit in these years as a few extra aches and pains might begin to creep in. Immobility, including sitting too often at work, driving when you could walk, slouching in front of the television, employing help cleaning or gardening when you could really do most of it yourself and reap the muscle rewards, driving right to the shop door when you could park a little further away and enjoy a little walk: all of these rob the body of opportunities for working against gravity, and it's fighting gravity that helps keep our muscles supporting our bodies and brains.

During these years, keep thinking of all the ways you can work your body against the effects of gravity, as well as doing exercise to maintain fitness.

70-plus

In these years, weight loss is to be avoided because of the muscle loss it causes. Instead, maintain the weight you have achieved already and stay as active as you possibly can.

The most important part of nutrition at this time of life is making sure you get enough protein and keeping up good muscle activity to maintain essential muscle reserve as discussed throughout this book. There is always benefit in eating colourful brain-protecting foods and those containing omega-3 along with that.

Nutrition is always a balancing act between what might be the best idea at the point in time and what might be a potential problem. The overriding and well-tested things that we know are of benefit to the brain are maintaining physical activity, doing regular exercise and eating foods that offer antioxidant and anti-inflammatory protection for brain cells as much as possible.

In these years it is *reduced* appetite and finding yourself *not* feeling hungry at mealtimes that is not only common, but potentially very dangerous. I, for one, can't imagine a time when I won't feel like eating most of the day, but it's something that is extremely common for all sorts of reasons as people move into their later years. Medications play a part in this, along with illness, social isolation, grief and a number of age-related changes in the digestive system.

Sometimes your body might make a mistake reading the hunger signs and tell you that you are not hungry when a mealtime comes along, or that you are full on a couple of mouthfuls.

‘ **Since most people tend to eat smaller meals later in life, each one must pack nutrients in.** ’

You need to realise that these 'I'm not hungry' signals are mistakes your hunger centre is making. Your brain needs a constant supply of nutrients and fuel and, since most people tend to eat smaller meals later in life, each one must pack nutrients in to provide it the support it needs.

The same applies to feelings of thirst. This is discussed in Chapter 4 also, so be aware that dehydration can occur more easily with advancing age and potentially create havoc for the brain. Anyone who is having issues with reduced appetite or has concerns for someone else should consult a doctor or a dietitian. You can also refer to my previous book, *Eat to Cheat Ageing*.

In these years, unintentional weight loss should never be seen as an advantage: it is potentially a sign of health issues, including dementia, so must be addressed and avoided.

PART TWO

the
Recipes

Pantry essentials

Putting a little thought into maintaining a well-stocked pantry is the best starting point to launch into better eating habits. A few hardworking ingredients mean you can create a delicious and nutritious meal quickly. This is important if you're cooking for one or you're too tired to cook anything more fancy than a piece of toast for dinner every night. Here is a list of things good to keep on hand, and you will find pretty much everything on it at your local supermarket or health-food store.

In the cupboard

Smart ingredients (and their benefits):

Spices

All spices contain antioxidants — they are what give them their colour and much of their flavour — and, as discussed in previous chapters of this book, many have been shown to also have helpful anti-inflammatory properties.

Do remember, though, that much of the talk you might hear about the benefits of turmeric (curcumin), cinnamon, rosemary and others usually is based on studies where the amounts used were well beyond what you could practically eat (usually given in tablet form), so the findings of these studies don't always apply to the amounts you might eat in foods.

It's also important to realise that, when any food component or herb is eaten in quantities way beyond what could usually be found in food, they behave more like medications than like food. Because of that, there can be consequences to your health from taking some of these in the amounts available in tablets. Many can interact with medications you might be taking, or affect your liver and other organs.

By contrast, when these are eaten in the amounts in these recipes, and especially when they have the chance to interact with other food components which balance or even enhance their benefits, there is plenty to be gained. While marketing claims or reports on individual research projects looking at one substance or another in isolation might promote the benefits of just that substance, medical research consistently indicates that eating a wide variety of different antioxidants and other food components that pack in the benefits is the key to getting the most from your food. These recipes using a wide array of delicious, fragrant spices will always be doing your brain some good.

Cinnamon

This excellent spice has had a bit of attention in recent years, having been found to assist in diabetes management and maintaining healthy cholesterol levels. For these reasons as well as the variety of antioxidants and anti-inflammatory substances it offers, there are also benefits for the brain. Be aware, though, that there are two main types of cinnamon on the market and they do have somewhat different properties. All are sold either as quills (sticks), which are rolled bark, or powdered.

'True' cinnamon (with the botanical name of *Cinnamomum verum*, but also known as *Cinnamomum zeylanicum*) comes mostly from Sri Lanka (it's sometimes still called Ceylon cinnamon despite that country's name change on becoming a republic more than 40 years ago!) and southern India. The bark is thin so the quill is many-layered and closely rolled, but is also quite fragile and can be easily broken up in your hand. In contrast, what is more commonly available is 'cassia' cinnamon (*Cinnamomum cassia*), usually from China, Vietnam or Indonesia: the bark is thicker and the quill is just one or two layers. It's not fragile and doesn't easily break in your hand.

When it comes to ground cinnamon, it's a bit difficult to know what type of cinnamon you are eating, as the labels don't always specify the source or the type; however, in nutritional

terms, it might not matter. You might read claims that only 'true' cinnamon is of benefit to the brain; however, many studies that have investigated the health benefits of cinnamon have used cassia cinnamon or didn't specify the type at all. So, the benefits have been shown from either type. Both contain valuable antioxidants and anti-inflammatory substances.

Many prefer to use 'true' cinnamon, but do be aware that it is more expensive and can be challenging to find in shops.

The only concern is that cassia cinnamon contains enough of a component that, when eaten in very large amounts by people already taking the medication warfarin, could cause excessive thinning of the blood and possibly contribute to liver damage in some people. The amounts you would need to eat to cause problems are far greater than you will use in the recipes in this book: a couple of teaspoons is great, but if you take it in tablet form (when the contents are compressed so extra is packed in) or have many spoonfuls during the day, problems might occur. As always, if you do choose to take any substance (including components of foods or herbs) in large amounts, discuss it with your doctor or pharmacist to ensure there is no conflict with medications you might be taking, or anything likely to interfere with your health.

In summary, look out for true cinnamon if you can get it, but if you can't, or are not sure, you can still enjoy the delicious flavour and the nutrient boost of the amount of cinnamon included in the recipes in this book.

Turmeric (curcumin)

This can be used fresh if you can get it (grate it straight into dishes or sprinkle on top), but ground turmeric is the one that is easy to keep in your pantry. This beautiful golden spice — best known in dishes from India, Pakistan, Morocco and the Middle East — is creating a bit of a stir in neuroscience research. The research being done uses much larger amounts than we would normally eat, so the benefits available from what's in these recipes are not quite the same; however, what we have here is a combination of this lovely spice with a variety of other ingredients that all contain antioxidant substances and ingredients that supply a number of valuable nutrients. Research has shown that turmeric needs fat or oil to be absorbed.

Cumin, coriander and fennel seeds

All of these seeds have plenty of antioxidants, along with the protein that is offered by all seeds. Keep whole seeds, as well as ground, if you have space for both. Freshly ground seeds tend to have a stronger flavour, so it's a great idea to keep whole seeds, dry roast them for a couple of minutes, then grind them as you need them using a mortar and pestle or spice grinder.

Paprika

This vibrant spice is the dried skin and flesh of capsicums (peppers); the flavour and colour depend on the varieties that are used and whether the capsicums have been smoked or not before drying and grinding. Most paprika you will buy in a grocery store will be either sweet, hot or smoked. The sweetness in the first comes only from the sugars naturally found in the capsicum. It is the perfect one for most dishes. The hot varieties incorporate some more chilli-like varieties to give extra zing, and then of course there is cayenne pepper, which is a type made from the hot and spicy cayenne capsicum. Smoked paprika is made from capsicums that have been smoked before

drying and grinding. They give many Spanish, Mexican and Moroccan dishes their warm and dusky flavour and unique appeal. Whichever paprika you choose, be assured that it is packed with antioxidants. As always, use the freshest you can get to ensure the best flavour.

Nuts and seeds

Walnuts are especially high in omega-3 fats, but all nuts contain protein, antioxidants and an array of useful brain-supporting nutrients, so keep a variety on hand; walnuts, almonds, hazelnuts (filberts), pine nuts, pecans; as well as seeds such as pumpkin, sesame, sunflower and poppy seeds. Both nuts and seeds store quite well; however, when you buy them, check use-by dates and try to use them promptly, as the oils they contain can degrade in time (particularly in light, warm places). If you are keeping them for a while and you live in a warm or tropical area, its useful to keep them in the fridge or a cool place but allow them to return to room temperature to eat them for the best flavour.

Grains, such as quinoa, wholemeal couscous, farro (spelt) and pearl barley

Quinoa is not technically a grain, it is a pseudo-cereal and has a nutritional profile that actually makes it superior to most grains commonly used. There are three varieties usually available: white, red and black and often you will find a mixture of all three. Nutritionally they are practically the same.

The seeds are coated with substances called saponins that help protect the plant from pests and diseases and you might read that these are 'toxic' to humans so that quinoa needs lots of

Vibrantly coloured turmeric, whether fresh, dried or ground, is creating a stir in neuroscience research.

washing to remove them before you can eat it. Saponins have a 'soapyness' when they dissolve in water so the rinsing process produces frothy water. It's often suggested that quinoa be rinsed till the water runs clear so you know the saponins are gone, but more recent thinking suggests that saponins might be helpful to human health so, while washing is certainly advisable and also helps to reduce the bitterness, you don't need to be as meticulous about washing as you might have read elsewhere.

Qunioa is predominantly a cold-climate crop although production is spreading. It has about twice the protein of rice and similar grains, and that protein is what is called 'complete' because, like animal foods, it contains all the essential amino acids: that's unique among plant foods. It's extra-high in fibre and, unlike most grains, it is a good source of a number of important minerals including iron and zinc.

We prefer red quinoa for its attractive colour and creamy flavour, and because it's a little quicker to cook, but you can substitute any quinoa you can find. Quinoa is now grown in Australia and many other countries (although it's native to South America): what's normally grown in Australia is the white variety. If you choose to substitute white for red and reduce your food miles by choosing a local product, or use the tricolour variety that's also available, be sure to follow the cooking directions on the packet so it's cooked to perfection.

Seaweed

This is a great staple to have on hand if you are preparing Japanese-style soups and other dishes, but finding it in shops can be a little challenging. The nori wraps used for sushi are generally made from a type of 'red' seaweed and are acceptable if you can get nothing else, but they don't provide the textural benefits of other seaweeds (which are usually sold dried), such as kombu, sea spaghetti, dulse, sea lettuce or purple laver that you might find in the gourmet section of the supermarket, online or in imported food stores. Any of these can be used in the recipes in this book.

A word of caution here, dear readers! Seaweed is a great source of the vital brain nutrient iodine, which is needed to produce the hormone thyroxine and is not found in many other foods; however, the body needs just the right amount. Too much is just as much of a problem — in fact, it's dangerous — as too little. So even though sushi is all the rage and there is lots of hype around seaweed products on the internet and elsewhere, eating too much is not a good idea. Sushi a few days a week and kombu in a soup here and there adds variety to your diet and gives you plenty of iodine. But be careful of having it too much more than that, especially as you move into your later years.

Tinned fish, such as salmon and tuna, sardines and anchovies

All tinned fish contains the same omega-3 fats as fresh varieties so having them in the pantry is always worthwhile. Buy 'pole and line caught' tuna if you can, because fishing practices used for other tuna are considered unsustainable by environmental protection agencies. Large-scale fishing operations can reduce ocean stocks, threatening future availability, and they damage ocean ecosystems and also often kill turtles, whales, dolphins and other marine species. Pole-and-line fishing reduces the impact.

Pantry staples, such as dried legumes, grains, seeds and nuts, can be stored in airtight containers ready for use.

WHICH COCOA SHOULD YOU BUY?

Despite what you might read, cocoa and cacao are not as different nutritionally as might be suggested. All cacao beans, after harvesting, undergo fermentation at high temperatures and drying in the tropical sun or in factories at around 60–65°C (140–150°F). It is mostly this heat fermentation that produces the flavours for which cocoa or cacao is prized, as well as increasing antioxidant levels in the beans.

After drying, beans may be roasted. Beans that are not roasted are called 'raw' by marketers and attract higher prices, though the heat fermentation and drying they have undergone probably means that term is something of a misnomer.

Dried beans (roasted or not) have their husks removed to produce cacao nibs (the inside of the dried bean) which can be packaged or milled.

The milling process creates heat naturally, due to friction, and that melts the fat in the nib (all cacao nibs are about half cocoa butter, which is a fat, and half cocoa solids) and the end result is a liquid called cocoa liquor. This can be used to make a variety of products, or it can undergo one further process that separates the cocoa butter from the solids, which are ground to a powder.

Beans are roasted to develop certain nuances of the chocolate flavour and are otherwise processed in exactly the same way as 'raw' (more accurately, fermented and dried, but not roasted) beans.

Dutch cocoa (also called alkalised or 'dutched') has an extra step in which the beans or the nibs are treated with an alkali to reduce the bitterness. It is darker in colour and has a somewhat smoother flavour, but unfortunately the alkalising treatment destroys a large number of the antioxidants.

Both raw cacao and (non-alkalised) unsweetened cocoa powder are high in a variety of antioxidants. It does seem that some of these, especially the phenolic compounds, are lost during drying, roasting and further processing, so the so-called 'raw' (unroasted) cacao has an advantage over the roasted cocoa. But it does tend to be more expensive and a bit more difficult to get hold of at your local shop. Rest assured that dried cacao beans start off with such high levels of these great brain boosters that even if some is lost, there is still plenty even in everyday cocoa.

Don't worry if you have read that milk reduces absorption of some of these little beauties; that is outdated thinking. More recent studies have shown that the effect is minimal. But of course, you can always use whichever milk (cow's milk, or substitute) you prefer to make delicious drinks such as the Super hot chocolate on page 212.

All large-scale fishing has the potential to do damage and, partly as a result of that, as well as keeping up with worldwide demand, farming of salmon and other seafood is now practised on a larger scale. All food industries — land or sea — have some impact on the area where the raw ingredients are sourced, whether that be in water usage, fertilisers and pesticides, pollution, reduction of future supply or much more. The Australian salmon industry, which mostly has access to pristine waters in Tasmania, has to deal with less impact from runoff of things like pesticides and fertilisers into waterways than is dealt with in northern hemisphere fisheries, but it has its challenges still. The producers work hard to balance keeping up with demand against possible environmental impacts.

Sweeteners, such as brown sugar, honey, golden syrup (light treacle) and molasses

Sugar has received lots of bad press over the years and it is true that refined sugar (ingredient lists in foods might include names such as sugar, white sugar, dextrose, glucose,

ne juice, corn
nvert sugar, high–
e or fructose
ther than energy
sugar is added to
onal value: you get
nd minerals in for
n and, when eaten
utes to obesity, but
hy gut. However,
ounts such as in
face it, anyone
whole diet of the
and Sweet Things
to be your best body
the same problem.
ıs pages, for older
ght, are frail or who
eat foods in this book
to get essential extra
n array of nutrients.
people consume
confectionery, sugary
every day and that is
ımended in this book.
Less 'refined' types of sugar — brown sugar,
maple syrup, molasses, golden syrup (light
treacle) — contain tiny amounts of some
minerals so have just a bit of an advantage (the
darker they are, the more extra nutrients they
contain) over granulated table sugar. But that
doesn't mean that having lots of those is good!

Pulses, such as red lentils, puy lentils, chickpeas, black beans, cannellini beans

Pulses are a great choice for plant-based
protein, but they are certainly not only for
vegetarians: pulses add fibre, are prebiotic
(containing nutrients that encourage the
growth of bacteria in the gut) so help support
brain health by improving gut health. They
contain a variety of important antioxidants and
minerals, too, and have about half the protein
of meat and fish (so serves will be bigger to get
the protein you need). All can easily be bought
dried or tinned. Both types store well: dried
ones just need to be soaked and precooked.

Some people have difficulty digesting
substances called galacto-oligosaccharides
(thankfully abbreviated to GOS) and fructans
that are found in pulses; as a result they suffer
pain and bloating when they eat them. If
you have this reaction, it's possible to reduce
the levels of these substances in a few simple
steps. These substances partly leach out during
soaking, so there are two options: either buy
tinned varieties and discard the liquid (that's
also where the salt is, so tossing it out has an
added advantage) and than rinse the beans
or lentils well.

Alternatively, soak dried pulses at least
overnight, preferably changing the soaking
water a couple of times so some of the GOS
and fructans are washed away. There will
always be some left, but these processes reduce
levels enough that, even if you have had
problems in the past, you may be able to enjoy
these little nutritional treasures. If you have had
issues, take it slowly – start with no more than
a quarter of a cup serving and see how that
goes before increasing the amount you eat.

LSA

LSA is an acronym for a ground mixture
of linseeds (flaxseeds), sunflower seeds and
almonds and is a powerhouse of nutritional
goodness. It's loaded with omega-3 fats, adds
a protein boost to many dishes, and is an
excellent source of probiotic dietary fibre to
help your brain as well as your digestive system.

In the fridge

Cheese, such as feta, cheddar, parmesan

Cheese is a high-protein food that supplies plenty of calcium. Some types, including 'blue' varieties and any made from unpasteurised milk, also provide 'good' bacteria to boost your gut health. It's also an easy snack on a cracker, on a sandwich or on a ploughman's platter. Cheese adds flavour to many dishes, and can be grated into soups and salads, used in an omelette, scattered over pasta dishes or baked sweet potato to add extra protein and calcium.

Butter (versus margarine)

You have read in Chapter 5 that foods which have undergone the fewest steps between their original source and the way they are eaten tend to help reduce chronic inflammation. This argument might be offered when it comes to butter, as it certainly has undergone far fewer steps in production than margarine. Butter contains antioxidants and adds flavour when cooking. Mixing it with olive oil if sautéeing or browning combines the flavour of butter with the anti-inflammatory benefits of the oil, which also stops the butter from burning.

Yoghurt

Greek-style yoghurt is the same as any other yoghurt, but some of the liquid whey is strained off so it is thicker and more concentrated. It's always important to look for labelling that specifies 'live cultures' or 'probiotic' or lists the bacteria the yoghurt contains; that way you know you are getting the goodness of the brain-assisting gut bacteria. Not only that, but yoghurt has a lovely flavour and can be used in both sweet and savoury dishes. Add it to soups, make a dip, or serve it with stewed fruits.

Oils, such as walnut oil, extra virgin olive oil, cold-pressed sesame oil, flaxseed (linseed) oil, macadamia oil, rice bran oil

The 'good' fats in these oils are so important for your brain that it is worth buying the best you can afford. 'First cold-pressed' and 'extra virgin' designate premium (usually produced in smaller amounts, so more expensive) oils. Have a couple of types on hand: I suggest using premium oils to drizzle over vegies, in salads, to dip good bread in or to make dips and snacks. Keep less expensive oils for cooking: all oil gives a great anti-inflammatory boost for just a few extra kilojoules (calories).

Some oils can be heat-sensitive and need to be stored in the fridge: these include walnut, flaxseed and macadamia oils. Olive oil and rice bran oil are shelf stable. If you store olive oil in the fridge, it may solidify; stand it on the shelf for a while before use and it's back to liquid.

Tahini

A paste made of ground sesame seeds, tahini contains the nutritional goodness of sesame seeds, which, like all seeds, are high in protein, contain fats good for the body and brain, and supply a variety of essential vitamins and minerals, including calcium. Store tahini in the fridge to help the oil it contains stay fresh.

Green (and red) salad leaves

The cornerstone of any nutritious diet, a bag of prewashed leafy greens, a bunch of kale, or a cos (romaine) lettuce is the foundation for so many meals and lots of recipes in this book. You can buy mixed lettuce that contains leaves of other colours than green alone, offering an extra antioxidant boost. Combine salad leaves with toasted nuts, feta and a dollop of mayonnaise; or dump a tin of tuna on top

of a pile of leaves for an instant high-protein salad; wilt baby spinach on top of a fried egg for breakfast; stuff greens into sandwiches; use a cos lettuce leaf instead of bread to wrap around sandwich fillings; or stir chopped kale through soups, stir-fries, noodles and pasta.

Whenever you eat, ask yourself, 'How can I add leafy greens and colour to this dish?'

There are lots of different varieties of these types of vegetables available: some are better cooked, such as spinach and kale, while good raw options include rocket (arugula) for a peppery kick in salads, and red mizuna, which is worth eating just for the pretty look alone.

Always have fresh leafy greens in your fridge: the more colour variety, the better.

LET'S TALK ABOUT SALT

Eating to help your brain is all about balance and, when it comes to salt, that is no exception. Eating too much salt contributes to things like hypertension (high blood pressure), stroke and transient ischaemic attacks (TIAs, also called mini-strokes), all of which can impact brain health. Most heart- and brain-health strategies advocate keeping salt intake to a minimum and this book is no exception. Some of the recipes in this book do use small amounts of salt, but you are not going to eat only those foods. Again, it comes down to balance: these recipes are not intended to be your whole day's eating plan and combining them with plenty of vegetables and fruits is important, as is keeping down your intake of commercial foods — takeaway (take-out) and prepackaged meals, commercial cakes, biscuits, pastries and snack foods — that have salt added during processing.

Remember that not all foods that are high in salt will taste 'salty': bread, many breakfast cereals, prepackaged meals and commercial baked goods can contribute as much, or more, than the salty snack and takeaway foods you already know to avoid.

Another important consideration is that it's not so much sodium itself that is the issue, but a high intake of salt upsets an important balance between sodium and the essential mineral, potassium. Eating plenty of foods that contain potassium, but are not also high in salt (sodium)

is key, and the great thing is that those foods are, by and large, the ones I recommend to form the basis of your eating plan: minimally processed vegetables, fruits, wholegrains, pulses, dairy foods, fish and meats can all contain potassium. Some foods are especially high in potassium: most yellow or orange fruits (particularly bananas and tropical fruits), dried fruits, tomatoes, legumes, lentils and dried beans of all types, dark green vegetables, potatoes, powdered milk, nuts and seeds, bran cereals and chocolate to name a few. Eating as many different vegetables, fruits and other foods that do not have salt added in their production will give you a potassium boost and help keep that sodium–potassium balance in line.

The taste for salt is an acquired one: if you are used to salty foods, cut down gradually to allow your taste buds to adapt to a lower intake. Conversely, if you don't usually add salt during cooking then foods with added salt will taste more 'salty' than you might like. The great advantage of preparing your own meals is that you can choose whether to add salt or not, both in the recipes in this book, in other recipes or at the table.

Of course, if you have medical issues and have been prescribed a low-salt diet, requiring you to use no salt at all in cooking, then naturally you need to adhere to that when preparing these recipes. Otherwise, the choice is yours to salt or not.

Tool kit

This is a culinary tool kit, filled with ingredients, shortcuts and flavours to help build your meals with good proteins, brain-enhancing fats and vital nutrients.

Establishing a few good habits can make all the difference to how we eat. Spend a couple of hours in the kitchen one day a week — really, it's just soaking beans, cooking grains, roasting vegetables, nothing terribly labour-intensive — and you'll have the ingredients on hand to make nutritious meals in minutes during the rest of the week.

Having a fridge full of cooked ingredients means that you can throw together a delicious meal quickly and simply. To cooked farro (spelt), lentils and prepared salad dressing, simply add salad greens and a protein such as a boiled egg, some tinned tuna or crumbled feta cheese. Add an extra drizzle of macadamia or olive oil and some toasted seeds and you have a quick and tasty meal.

When doing your weekly shop, focus on three or four vegetables and fruits that are in season, and of different colours. Don't try to fill your fridge with dozens of ingredients that you're not going to eat. For example, in winter go for a red cabbage, orange sweet potato, leafy greens, red onions and a cauliflower. In summer, opt for all the coloured tomatoes, cucumbers, capsicums (peppers) and zucchini (courgettes). Eat summer fruits such as yellow peaches, blueberries, red grapes, dark purple plums. In winter, go for green kiwifruit, green apples, red pears, orange citrus.

Think about your old favourites and how you can enhance their nutritional profile. For breakfast, poach an egg and serve it on toast with some wilted spinach, a handful of savoury granola, chopped avocado and half a tomato. Instead of a cheese sandwich for lunch, apply a thick smear of cauliflower dip, some crunchy grated carrot and a generous handful of coloured lettuce. For dinner, think about putting as many coloured vegetables on your plate as possible — 'eat the rainbow' — and swap mashed potato for mashed sweet potato sometimes, swap pasta for quinoa, wholemeal couscous or farro sometimes. Even just adding more colour to your plate with some thinly sliced red cabbage, sliced tomato or diced avocado, a handful of toasted pumpkin seeds (pepitas) along with a drizzle of a good-quality olive or nut oil to your favourite dishes can go a long way towards increasing the brain benefits of what you eat.

To set yourself up for the week, pick two or three of the following basic foods to prepare and store in the fridge. They'll make it easy for you to quickly throw together a power-packed meal with minimum effort for busy times.

Start chopping

As soon as you get home from your weekly shop spend a little time preparing vegetables before you put them away. Cut cauliflower and broccoli into florets, shred some red cabbage, remove the woody stems from kale leaves before storing in airtight containers. A little time preparing your vegetables will make your weeknight cooking much quicker (although this doesn't work with vegetables that will turn brown, such as potatoes).

While we're on the topic of chopping, a mandolin is worth investing in, because you can thinly slice vegetables, making them easier to eat raw, which is tastier and so you'll be inclined to eat more of them. A mandolin can seem a little scary at first, but using one to slice vegetables such as cabbage and radishes can take ordinary vegetables to new culinary heights.

A word on storage
Nuts and seeds keep better in the fridge, and so do whole grains, if it's practical. Really oily nuts such as macadamias can be frozen. The oils can turn rancid very quickly so buy them in small amounts and quickly use them up. Stale nuts aren't going to taste good. Salads are usually best served at room temperature, so bear that in mind when preparing your meals. And please don't store your tomatoes in the fridge, they don't like it.

Cook quinoa
Quinoa is coated in a bitter substance called saponins, and you'll need to wash this off before cooking. The best way is to actually soak the quinoa in acidulated water (water with lemon juice added) for 12 hours first, then cook as you would for rice, or if you're short on time, give it a good rinse under the tap and cook it as usual.

Soak quinoa in water overnight or, if you're short on time, it's okay to just rinse it under the tap.

Quinoa is cooked when little spirals come out of the grains. Fluff it with a fork and store or serve.

The absorption method is best; and remember, one cup of quinoa grains makes three cups of cooked quinoa. Rinse 200 g (7 oz/1 cup) of soaked quinoa under running water and tip into a large saucepan over medium heat. Stir around the pan to dry out the grains. Continue to cook the quinoa until it starts to turn a golden colour, smells toasty and the little seeds start to pop, after about 2 minutes. Add 500 ml (17 fl oz/2 cups) of water (or stock) and bring to the boil, then reduce to a simmer, cover and cook for 15 minutes or until the liquid has absorbed and little spirals come out of the grains. Remove from the heat and stand for 5 minutes before fluffing the grains with a fork. Store in an airtight container in the fridge for up to 5 days, or in the freezer for up to 2 months.

Cook beans

Tinned beans are a convenient and nutritious staple to keep in your pantry, but cooking your own beans from scratch is not only cheaper but much tastier. You can cook them for much longer so they absorb all the flavours from your soups and sauces, and sometimes tinned beans can have an unpleasant 'tinned' flavour, which you avoid if cooking from dried. Cooking from dried also means more flavour and less mush; however, old dried beans lose their flavour and can take ages to cook, and often don't cook evenly. So check the use-by date when buying dried beans: you generally want them to be less than a year old when you use them.

To cook beans, soak for 24 hours in water, up to 48 hours if you have time. Drain the beans and refill with clean water a couple of times. Changing the water helps reduce the amount of some substances in dried beans that can cause abdominal pain and bloating. It's

Soak dried beans for 24–48 hours in water, draining and refilling with clean water a couple of times.

normal and good to produce some wind — it actually shows that gut bacteria are doing their job! — but if that causes excessive pain or distress it's worth soaking repeatedly and tossing the water out each time.

Drain the beans, put them in a saucepan and cover with plenty of cold water. Add a teaspoon of salt, and some aromatics such as bay leaves, garlic cloves, peppercorns or thyme sprigs. Simmer the beans until tender, topping up the water if it gets low. This can take anywhere from 30 minutes to an hour or two depending on the age of the beans and how long you've soaked them. When testing beans, taste two or three, as sometimes they cook unevenly and one might be ready when the rest are still a little crunchy. Drain the beans, discard any aromatics and store the beans in the fridge for up to 4 days or freeze in resealable plastic bags for up to 6 months.

Puy lentils, sometimes called French or green lentils, are best for salads. They hold their shape when cooked. Red lentils are good for curries and soups, as they quickly break down and thicken your dishes. To cook lentils, soak them in water for 24 hours, rinsing and changing the water if you remember, and then cook them in a large saucepan of water (salt the water if you like) until tender. Adding whole crushed garlic cloves, a piece of ginger or a small onion cut in half to the cooking water will really add some extra flavour.

Cook chickpeas (garbanzo beans)

To prepare chickpeas, put 200 g (7 oz/1 cup) of dried chickpeas in a large bowl, big enough to allow room for the peas to expand. Cover with water and soak for 24 hours, changing the water at least once. Drain and rinse the chickpeas, transfer to a saucepan and cover with fresh water or stock to a depth of 4 cm (1¾ inches). Add aromatics such as rosemary, garlic or ginger; a piece of seaweed such as kombu or wakame will add extra flavour and nutrients. Simmer the chickpeas for 20–40 minutes until tender (the time really depends on the age of the chickpeas). Store the cooked chickpeas in their cooking water for up to 3 days in an airtight container in the fridge.

Toast nuts

Nuts on their own are a delicious and satisfying snack; however, toasting the nuts will add crunch to their texture and enhance their flavour by releasing their oils. Toasting nuts is pretty straightforward, although you need to keep an eye on them, as there's only about a minute between perfectly toasted and perfectly burnt. Using a timer is recommended!

Preheat the oven to 180°C (350°F). Spread the nuts in a single layer on a baking tray lined with baking paper and put them in the oven. Check after 10 minutes and give the tray a shake to toss the nuts. Cook for another 5 minutes or until golden and the nuts smell fragrant (you might hear them cracking). Smaller nuts such as pine nuts cook really quickly, in around 5 minutes, but larger nuts like almonds, hazelnuts (filberts) and walnuts will take closer to 15 minutes. Once they are cool, store in an airtight container, and eat them within 7–10 days for maximum flavour. You can freeze toasted nuts, too; simply bring back to room temperature before eating.

Toast nuts on a baking tray lined with baking paper in the oven, then store them in an airtight container.

Spicy mixed seeds

A little jar of spicy mixed seeds is a versatile nutritional tool to have at your fingertips. Scatter on salads, soups or roasted vegetables. They also make a delicious predinner snack and are a good alternative to chips (crisps).

MAKES ABOUT 1 CUP

40 g (1½ oz/¼ cup) sunflower seeds

40 g (1½ oz/¼ cup) sesame seeds

40 g (1½ oz/¼ cup) flaxseeds (linseeds)

40 g (1½ oz/¼ cup) pumpkin seeds (pepitas)

1 teaspoon ground cumin

2 teaspoons ground coriander

½ teaspoon ground turmeric

¼ teaspoon smoked paprika

½ teaspoon salt

1 tablespoon rice bran oil

Preheat the oven to 160°C (315°F). Mix all of the ingredients in a small bowl. Spread out on a baking tray lined with baking paper and roast for 15–20 minutes or until dry and golden. Stir halfway through the cooking time. Allow to cool before storing in an airtight jar.

Sweet dukkah

Sweet dukkah takes the popular seed and spice mix and adds sugar and spices to create a seasoning for yoghurt, ice cream and stewed fruits such as apples or pears.

MAKES ABOUT 2 CUPS

250 g (9 oz/1⅔ cups) sesame seeds

125 g (4½ oz) hazelnuts (filberts)

60 g (2¼ oz) ground cinnamon

20 g (¾ oz) ground cardamom

20 g (¾ oz) unsweetened cocoa powder

1 teaspoon icing (confectioners') sugar

Preheat the oven to 200°C (400°F). Put the seeds and nuts on separate baking trays (lined with baking paper) and roast them for 5–10 minutes or until they begin to colour and release an aroma.

Remove from the oven and put them into a food processor with the remaining ingredients and process until they are finely crushed but not pulverised. Be careful not to overblend or the oil from the too finely ground seeds and nuts will form a paste. Dukkah should be a dry crushed mixture, not a paste.

Store for up to 3 months in an airtight container in the fridge.

Savoury granola

These nutty savoury clusters pack a nutritional punch and are delicious on soups, salads or over a fried egg in the morning.

MAKES ABOUT 2 CUPS

1 eggwhite, lightly beaten

60 g (2¼ oz) almonds

60 g (2¼ oz/½ cup) walnuts

60 g (2¼ oz) pistachios

120 g (4¼ oz) rolled (porridge) oats

60 g (2¼ oz) pumpkin seeds (pepitas)

30 g (1 oz) sesame seeds

60 ml (2 fl oz/¼ cup) olive oil

2 tablespoons ground cumin

2 tablespoons dried thyme

1 teaspoon salt

1 teaspoon pepper

Preheat the oven to 180°C (350°F). Line a baking tray with baking paper. Mix everything together in a large bowl, then spread the mixture in a thin layer over the prepared tray. Bake for 10–15 minutes, stirring once, until golden. Set aside to cool. Store in an airtight container for up to 2 weeks.

4-ingredient tahini dressing

Okay, five ingredients if you include the salt, but who's counting? This is really great on cabbage, with salad leaves or avocado.

MAKES ABOUT ¾ CUP

65 g (2½ oz/¼ cup) tahini, or a little less for a runnier consistency

60 ml (2 fl oz/¼ cup) apple cider vinegar

60 ml (2 fl oz/¼ cup) extra virgin olive oil

2 tablespoons sesame oil

pinch of salt (optional)

Mix the ingredients together in a small bowl. Season with extra salt if required. Store for up to 7 days in an airtight container in the fridge.

Salad dressing

Simple is best, so make a jar of this dressing and store it in your fridge to keep your salads well dressed for the week.

MAKES ABOUT 2 CUPS

40 g (1½ oz) dijon mustard

80 ml (2½ fl oz/⅓ cup) apple cider vinegar

350 ml (12 fl oz) olive oil

sea salt and black pepper

Blitz the mustard and vinegar in a blender. With the motor running, slowly add the olive oil until the dressing emulsifies. Season to taste. Store in a large airtight jar in the fridge. Shake before using.

Quick mayonnaise

So much better than any store-bought version, this keeps in a jar in the fridge for up to a week. Use it on sandwiches, salads or on the fish cakes on page 172. A teaspoon of mayonnaise is a simple way to add good fats and protein to your meal.

MAKES ABOUT 1½ CUPS

1 tablespoon dijon mustard

2 eggs

1 teaspoon salt (or to taste)

pinch of sugar

2 tablespoons apple cider vinegar

125 ml (4 fl oz/½ cup) macadamia oil

125 ml (4 fl oz/½ cup) olive oil

In a food processor, process the mustard, eggs, salt, sugar and vinegar for about 30 seconds until smooth.

With the motor running, add the macadamia oil through the feed tube in a very slow trickle. This step should take about 1 minute. Once the mixture is emulsified and thick, pour in the olive oil and continue to process until glossy and thick. Season with extra salt if required.

Vegetable stock

Vegetable stock is a useful tool to have on hand, so make a big pot and freeze it in 500 ml (17 fl oz/2 cup) portions. Use for soups or to cook beans or quinoa.

MAKES ABOUT 4 LITRES

1 tablespoon butter

1 tablespoon olive oil

1 fennel bulb, including tops, coarsely chopped

2 brown onions, unpeeled, cut into quarters

6 carrots, cut into thirds

1 leek, white and green parts, cut into thirds

3 celery stalks, including the leaves, coarsely chopped

1 small sweet potato, washed and coarsely chopped

1 large bunch of flat-leaf (Italian) parsley

6 thyme sprigs

2 rosemary sprigs

6 garlic cloves, smashed

2 thumb-size pieces of ginger, cut in half lengthways

12 black peppercorns

2 bay leaves

1 teaspoon salt (optional)

Melt the butter and olive oil in a large, heavy-based saucepan. Add the fennel, onions, carrots, leek, celery, sweet potato, parsley, thyme, rosemary, garlic and ginger and cook over medium heat until vegetables start to colour. Add the peppercorns and bay leaves, then add 4 litres (140 fl oz/16 cups) of water. Cover with a lid and bring to a gentle boil. Remove the lid, reduce the heat to low and simmer, uncovered, for 2–4 hours. As the broth simmers, some of the liquid will evaporate, so top up with a little more water if the vegetables begin to peek out. Remove from the heat and allow to cool slightly, then strain the stock through a colander into a bowl and discard the solids. Let cool to room temperature before refrigerating for up to 1 week or freezing for up to 3 months.

Quick pickle

Pickles are a super-versatile condiment: they add so much flavour to a dull sandwich, a tired salad, even as a tasty little morsel on the side of your dinner plate. The vinegar kickstarts your taste buds and gets your appetite going and, well, they're made of vegetables which must be good. There are loads of vegetables to choose from that can be pickled. This pickling solution is more of a blueprint for creating your own favourite flavour combinations with additional ingredients such as dried chilli and fennel seeds, mustard seeds and bay leaves, or dill seeds and garlic. These quick pickles are designed to be kept in the fridge and eaten within a week.

MAKES ABOUT 2 CUPS

125 ml (4 fl oz/½ cup) apple cider vinegar

1 teaspoon sugar

½ teaspoon black peppercorns

1 teaspoon salt

vegetables, such as radishes, green tomatoes, red cabbage, zucchini (courgette) or cucumber, thinly sliced

aromatics, such as thyme, rosemary or bay leaves

In a small saucepan, gently heat the vinegar, sugar, peppercorns and salt with 125 ml (4 fl oz/½ cup) of water until it starts to simmer. Simmer for 5 minutes to allow the flavours to infuse.

Meanwhile, pack a clean jar with sliced vegetables, layering any aromatics you might like to add such as thyme leaves, rosemary or bay leaves. Pour the hot vinegar solution over the vegetables, seal with the lid and allow to cool to room temperature, then store in the fridge. Stand for a day before eating.

COOKING *for* ONE *or* TWO

Cooking for one can be just as delicious and satisfying as cooking for a crowd. Single serve recipes in this chapter can easily be doubled to serve two people.

Middle Eastern fried eggs

The excellent protein of eggs combines with a smattering of spices, spinach and tomato, offering antioxidants including lutein. Finish with any fresh herbs you like, we've used flat-leaf (Italian) parsley but coriander, mint or a combination is delicious too.

SERVES 1

1 tablespoon butter

1 garlic clove, crushed

½ teaspoon ground cumin

1 teaspoon ground coriander

½ teaspoon salt

½ teaspoon pepper

2 eggs

handful of baby spinach

1 small tomato, chopped

handful of flat-leaf (Italian) parsley, coarsely chopped, to serve

flatbread, to serve (optional)

In a large heavy-based frying pan, melt the butter over medium–low heat then add the garlic and cook for about 1 minute until softened: you don't want it to go brown at all. Add the spices and cook for a few moments until they start to sizzle and smell fragrant.

Crack the eggs into the spicy butter mix and gently cook until set, spooning melted spicy butter over to cook the tops.

Move the eggs to one side, add the spinach and toss in the hot butter until wilted. This should take about 60 seconds.

To serve, place the spinach on a plate, top with the eggs, pour on any remaining melted butter from the pan, add the diced tomato, chopped parsley and serve with flatbread (if using). Alternatively, simply add the tomato and parsley to the spinach and eggs and serve in the pan on a heatproof trivet.

Smart sardines and tomato on toast

A classic standby dish that still has merit and deserves to be included. Sardines, like all oily fish, are a great source of marine omega-3 fats, balanced with the antioxidant boost of parsley, tomato, rocket (arugula) and lemon juice.

SERVES 1

1 tin sardines, drained

1 small tomato, finely chopped

handful of flat-leaf (Italian) parsley, chopped

1 tablespoon good-quality mayonnaise (see recipe on page 83)

a few drops of Tabasco sauce

2 tablespoons lemon juice

2 wholegrain sourdough bread slices, toasted and buttered

handful of rocket (arugula) leaves

olive oil, for drizzling

lemon wedges, to serve

In a small bowl, crush the sardines with a fork, then add the tomato, parsley, mayonnaise, Tabasco sauce and lemon juice and gently stir to combine.

Pile the sardines onto the buttered toast, then top with the rocket leaves, drizzle with olive oil and serve with lemon wedges and freshly ground black pepper.

Yoghurt and savoury granola

A delicious combination of the probiotic offerings of good-quality yoghurt, extra protein from eggs, nuts and LSA, and all those fabulous colours and good oils for antioxidants and their anti-inflammatory benefits. Inspired by the classic Turkish breakfast, it's a refreshing breakfast (or any time of the day really), especially in summer when tomatoes are at their best.

SERVES 1

130 g (4½ oz/½ cup) probiotic Greek-style yoghurt

pinch of ground turmeric

½ Lebanese (short) cucumber, chopped

3–4 cherry tomatoes, halved

handful of small black olives

1 tablespoon LSA

handful of chopped flat-leaf (Italian) parsley

a few chives, chopped

2 tablespoons savoury granola (see page 81) or handful of almonds, toasted and chopped

1 soft-boiled egg, peeled

olive oil, macadamia or flaxseed oil, to drizzle

salt flakes (optional) and freshly ground black pepper

Spoon the yoghurt in the bottom of a serving bowl or plate and sprinkle with turmeric. Arrange the cucumber, tomato and olives over the yoghurt. Sprinkle the LSA over the top, then scatter the herbs and granola over. Cut the egg in half and place in the centre. An extra drizzle of oil is nice, then season with salt flakes (if using) and freshly ground black pepper.

Dukkah-crusted salmon with quick couscous salad

A vibrant combination of coloured foods and spices for antioxidants; brain-boosting anti-inflammatory omega-3 fats from salmon, nuts and good cooking oils; topped off with a bonus bit of probiotic goodness from good-quality Greek-style yoghurt. Dukkah is a classic Middle Eastern spice mix, readily available in supermarkets. Look for types that contain a variety of nuts, spices and seeds. Sumac is a ground berry with a tangy lemon flavour and is delicious with fish.

SERVES 1

200 g (7 oz) salmon fillet, skin on

good-quality but neutral-flavoured nut or seed oil, such as rice bran oil, for coating and frying

2 tablespoons dukkah

1 tablespoon yoghurt

squeeze of lemon juice

pinch of salt

½ teaspoon sumac

SALAD

couscous for one (see below)

handful of flat-leaf (Italian) parsley, chopped

3 cherry tomatoes, halved

55 g (2 oz) green beans, cooked

1 dried apricot, finely chopped

zest and juice of ½ lemon

1 tablespoon pine nuts, toasted

1 spring onion (scallion), thinly sliced

1 tablespoon olive oil

To make the salad, combine all of the ingredients in a small bowl and set aside.

Rub the salmon fillet with rice bran oil, then cover the skin generously with the dukkah.

Heat a heavy-based frying pan over high heat and add a little rice bran oil. Carefully place the salmon, skin-side down, in the pan and cook for 1 minute (don't cook this side any longer or the dukkah will burn). Turn the salmon over and cook for a further 3–4 minutes. Thin the yoghurt with the lemon juice and mix in the salt and sumac. Serve the salmon alongside the couscous salad and drizzle with the yoghurt dressing.

Couscous for one

50 g (1¾ oz/¼ cup) couscous

¼ teaspoon salt

In a small saucepan, bring 80 ml (2½ fl oz/⅓ cup) of water to the boil. Stir in the couscous and salt. Remove from the heat: cover with a lid and stand for about 5 minutes, until the water has been absorbed. Before serving, fluff with a fork.

Hot-smoked salmon and potato salad with crème fraîche

What a brain-boosting combination: the probiotic and prebiotic benefits of sauerkraut with the omega-3 of salmon, anti-inflammatory extra virgin olive oil, and a bit of extra protein from eggs. Commonly called a Scandi salad, as it's inspired by the smoked fish dishes of Scandinavia, this is a substantial meal and it's really easy to prepare. It's good with any smoked fish you can find, so try trout or herring if you can get your hands on them.

SERVES 1

3–4 baby potatoes, scrubbed but skin left on

200 g (7 oz) green beans, washed and trimmed

handful of green salad leaves

2 tablespoons olive oil

1 tablespoon lemon juice

100 g (3½ oz) hot-smoked salmon

1 soft-boiled egg, peeled and quartered

1 radish, thinly sliced

1 tablespoon sauerkraut

2 tablespoons crème fraîche

a few dill sprigs

¼ teaspoon dill seeds

Put the baby potatoes in a small saucepan, cover with cold water and bring to the boil over high heat. Reduce heat to a simmer, add salt if you wish and cook gently for about 15 minutes until the potatoes are tender. Drain and set aside. When cool enough to handle, cut in half and set aside.

In a large saucepan of boiling water, cook the beans for 8 minutes or until just tender. Drain and plunge the beans into a bowl of iced water to stop the cooking process and maintain the bright green colour. Once the beans are cold, drain, pat dry and set aside.

To serve, combine the salad leaves and potatoes in a bowl and toss with half the olive oil and lemon juice, season with salt and pepper, then arrange on a serving plate. Use your fingers to break the salmon into large chunks and scatter over the salad. Arrange the egg, sliced radish and green beans over the salad.

Drizzle with the remaining olive oil and lemon juice.

Add the sauerkraut to the side. Spoon on a generous amount of crème fraîche, scatter the dill sprigs on top and finish with a sprinkling of dill seeds.

Quick 'baked' beans with bacon and eggs

Not exactly 'baked', but a quick stovetop version of the slow-baked variety. Nevertheless, the beans in this dish offer protein while also contributing a prebiotic and anti-inflammatory boost. They can be enjoyed alone as a vegetarian and vegan option, or with the added protein of the egg, bacon and feta. The molasses or treacle provides flavourful sweetness to this classic dish. This recipe makes enough for at least two serves of baked beans, depending on how hungry you are. If cooking for one, halve the amount of bacon, egg and cheese but make the same amount of the beans. You can store the leftover beans in an airtight container in the fridge for up to 4 days.

SERVES 2

splash of olive oil

1 teaspoon ground coriander

½ teaspoon ground cumin

1 teaspoon smoked paprika

400 g (14 oz) tin crushed tomatoes

400 g (14 oz) tin cannellini beans, rinsed and drained

1 tablespoon molasses or treacle

2 bacon slices

2 eggs

2 tablespoons crumbled feta cheese

a few coriander (cilantro) leaves

In a large saucepan, heat the olive oil over medium heat and add the spices. As soon as they become fragrant add the crushed tomatoes and beans. Increase the heat, bring to the boil then reduce heat and simmer for 10 minutes, stirring occasionally. Add the molasses and stir through then cook for another minute or two. Remove from heat and set aside.

Fry the bacon and eggs to your liking. To serve, divide the beans into two bowls, add an egg and a bacon slice to each, then top with the feta and scatter with coriander leaves.

Roasted pumpkin salad with walnuts, rocket and chorizo

The beautiful natural sweetness and antioxidants of pumpkin are boosted by the omega-3 fats of walnuts, pumpkin seeds (pepitas), a bit of extra zing and protein from chorizo, all topped off with the antioxidant and anti-inflammatory contributions of nutmeg, rosemary, garlic and olive oil. Whack all these ingredients into the oven and forget about them for a while. Dinner's ready in half an hour.

SERVES 2

½ butternut pumpkin (squash), about 500 g (1 lb 2 oz), cut into 2 cm (¾ inch) wedges

½ teaspoon ground nutmeg

4 garlic cloves, smashed

1 rosemary sprig, chopped

1 whole chorizo, sliced about 1 cm (⅜ inch) thick

2 tablespoons olive oil, plus 60 ml (2 fl oz/¼ cup) extra

1 tablespoon lemon juice

handful of rocket (arugula)

2 tablespoons walnuts, toasted

2 tablespoons pumpkin seeds (pepitas), toasted

Preheat the oven to 180°C (350°F). Line a baking tray with baking paper.

Put the pumpkin, nutmeg, garlic and rosemary into a large bowl, drizzle with the olive oil and toss well to mix. Tumble onto the prepared baking tray in a single layer.

Roast in the oven for 15 minutes, then remove the tray, turn the pumpkin slices over and add the sliced chorizo. Return the tray to the oven and cook for a further 10 minutes or until the pumpkin is soft and golden brown.

Whisk together the extra olive oil and lemon juice in a small bowl and season with salt and pepper.

Toss the cooked pumpkin mixture with rocket and walnuts, pile into a serving bowl and drizzle with the olive oil and lemon juice dressing. Scatter with pumpkin seeds and serve.

Cauliflower pizza with tomato, rocket and goat's cheese

Cauliflower pizza has a bit of a buzz about it lately, but it's so delicious! Here is a dish that is not only a great option for coeliacs, who need to avoid gluten, but also brings the versatility of pizza to a new level, adding the benefits of cauliflower to one of our favourite meals. There are plenty of antioxidants and anti-inflammatory properties in cauliflower and tomato, plus protein from cheese and eggs. You can also use the cauliflower 'rice' instead of regular rice with curries and stir-fries.

SERVES 2

½ cauliflower, coarsely chopped

1 teaspoon salt

2 eggs, beaten

100 g (3½ oz) ricotta cheese

100 g (3½ oz/1 cup) ground almonds

olive oil, to drizzle

2 tablespoons goat's cheese

6 cherry tomatoes, halved

1 tablespoon grated parmesan cheese

handful of rocket (arugula) leaves

handful of basil leaves

Preheat the oven to 200°C (400°F). Line a baking tray with baking paper and set aside.

To make the cauliflower 'rice', pulse batches of raw cauliflower florets in a food processor until it resembles rice.

Put about 2 cm (¾ inch) of water into a large saucepan and bring it to the boil. Add the cauliflower 'rice' and salt, cover and cook for 4–5 minutes. Drain through a fine strainer and continue to allow to drain and cool for about 10 minutes. Once cool enough to handle, wrap in a tea towel (dish towel) and squeeze over the sink to get rid of as much liquid as you can. The cauliflower will release a lot of liquid and you need to remove as much as possible so your pizza isn't soggy.

Transfer to a clean bowl: it should feel dry and look like rice. Add the egg, ricotta and ground almonds to the cauliflower. Mix well with your hands to combine.

Press the dough out in a disc on the prepared baking tray. Keep the disc about 1 cm (⅜ inch) thick, and make the edges a little higher for a crust effect. Bake for 35–40 minutes. It should be firm and golden brown when ready.

Drizzle with olive oil, then top with the goat's cheese, tomato and parmesan. Return to the oven for a few minutes until cheese is melted and golden. Scatter with rocket and basil leaves and season with salt and pepper if desired. Serve immediately.

Roasted chickpea tzatziki salad wraps

Protein as well as prebiotics from these delicious pulses combine with the anti-inflammatory benefits of the spices, oil and herbs. Top that off with some probiotic yoghurt and crisp colourful salad, and this is a winning dish. You can roast the chickpeas ahead of time and keep them in an airtight container. Make a double batch, as the roasted chickpeas make a tasty high-protein snack.

SERVES 2

1 cup cooked chickpeas
(see page 78)

1 teaspoon ground cumin

1 teaspoon ground turmeric

1 teaspoon smoked paprika

pinch of cayenne pepper

1 teaspoon freshly ground
black pepper

juice of ½ lemon

1 tablespoon olive oil

4 pita pockets, halved

1 large tomato, chopped

1 small cos (romaine) lettuce,
roughly chopped

1 Lebanese (short) cucumber,
finely chopped

handful of fresh mint leaves,
finely chopped

YOGHURT DRESSING

260 g (9¼ oz/1 cup) Greek-style
yoghurt

1 teaspoon finely chopped mint

1 garlic clove, finely chopped

Preheat the oven to 180°C (350°F). Line a baking tray with baking paper.

In a large mixing bowl, combine the chickpeas, spices, lemon juice and olive oil, and use your hands to thoroughly coat the chickpeas with the spices.

Spread the coated chickpeas on the prepared baking tray, in one layer with a little space around each one so they crisp up. Roast the chickpeas for 20 minutes or until golden. Give the tray a little shake every now and then to make sure all the sides are coated. Once the chickpeas are done, remove them from the oven and set aside to cool.

Meanwhile, make the yoghurt dressing by mixing all of the ingredients in a small bowl. Season with salt and set aside.

To assemble, take one pita pocket half and start filling with a dollop of yoghurt dressing. Scoop a big spoonful of chickpeas onto the yoghurt. Top with the tomato, lettuce and cucumber. Finish with more yoghurt dressing and scatter the chopped mint leaves on the top.

You can also serve this dish in a bowl: start with the salad vegetables, then top with the chickpeas and yoghurt dressing, then serve with pita on the side or toasted and crumbled on top.

Red potato and ricotta pancake with smoked salmon and quick pickled radish

Try to find red-skinned potatoes: don't peel them, as you'll get the added benefits of the anthocyanin antioxidants in that lovely red skin. There is good protein in this dish from the ricotta and salmon, along with some bonus omega-3 fats. The zing of the pickle tops this dish off nicely.

SERVES 1

1 tablespoon caster (superfine) sugar

60 ml (2 fl oz/¼ cup) apple cider vinegar

60 ml (2 fl oz/¼ cup) hot water

4 radishes

2 red-skinned potatoes, such as pontiac, scrubbed but skin left on

2 spring onions (scallions), sliced

handful of dill, chopped, reserving 1 sprig for serving

2 tablespoons ricotta cheese

olive oil, for frying

80 g (2¾ oz) smoked salmon

1 tablespoon crème fraîche or sour cream

handful of green salad leaves

First make the pickle. In a small bowl, dissolve the caster sugar in the vinegar and hot water. Slice the radishes and put them in the bowl, making sure they're covered by the pickling liquid, then set aside.

Grate the potato, wrap it in a clean tea towel (dish towel) and squeeze out excess moisture. Transfer to a mixing bowl and add the spring onion, dill and ricotta. Season with plenty of salt and pepper and mix well to combine.

Heat a medium frying pan over medium heat, add a drizzle of olive oil, then pour the potato mixture into the hot oil. Smooth into a pancake shape about 1 cm (⅜ inch) thick. Reduce the heat and cook gently until the underside is golden, then carefully flip to cook the other side.

Place the potato pancake on a serving plate and top with the salmon, crème fraîche and drained pickled radish on the side. Add a handful of salad leaves, decorate with the reserved dill sprig and serve.

QUICK
power
MEALS

The idea behind these recipes is to provide you with some meals that you can quickly prepare and that are packed with brain goodies. Even if you go off the rails the rest of the day, you can get back on track if you've tucked into one of these.

Quinoa bowl with avocado

Packed with protein from quinoa, pumpkin seeds and the egg, plus plenty of good fats and antioxidants: if you've prepared your quinoa ahead, this dish is ready in minutes.

SERVES 1

½ cup cooked red quinoa (see page 76), warm or at room temperature

2–3 small yellow or red cherry tomatoes, quartered

½ ripe avocado, peeled and sliced

1 tablespoon pumpkin seeds (pepitas), toasted

1 egg, poached or fried

1 tablespoon LSA

handful of coriander (cilantro) leaves

Put the cooked quinoa in a cereal bowl, then add tomatoes, avocado and pumpkin seeds, arranged in neat piles or rows. Add the poached egg, top with coriander and sprinkle with LSA.

Haloumi breakfast bowl

Remember the hearty breakfast fry-up? Here's an updated version filled with all the good things your brain will thank you for, to start your day. Just add coffee and the paper.

SERVES 1

2 teaspoons butter for frying, plus extra if frying egg

2 tablespoons olive oil, plus extra for frying haloumi

25 g (1 oz/1 cup) kale leaves (stalks removed, sliced)

2 haloumi cheese slices

½ tomato

1 egg

1 teaspoon turmeric (optional)

¼ teaspoon pepper (optional)

1 tablespoon sesame seeds, black or white or a mixture of both

In a medium frying pan, melt the butter with the olive oil until sizzling then add the kale and a tiny splash of water. Fry for about 10 minutes until nice and soft. Remove from the heat and transfer to a shallow bowl.

Add a little more oil to the frying pan over medium heat and fry the haloumi on one side of the pan and the tomato on the other until both are nicely browned. Place neatly beside the kale in the bowl. Tip any tomato juices into the bowl.

Poach or fry the egg. To fry the egg, add a little extra butter to the frying pan, then crack the egg into the pan and sprinkle with the turmeric and pepper. Cook until the egg white is set, spooning the hot butter over the egg yolk to cook the top.

Add the poached or fried egg to the cereal bowl, sprinkle with sesame seeds and serve.

Rocket and farro Greek salad

First cultivated 2000 years ago, pearled farro (spelt) is an ancient grain related to wheat, that is also called emmer wheat in some places. Even though pearled farro has had the bran layer mostly removed, it's still quite high in fibre and remains a good source of protein, some B vitamins and the mineral zinc. More importantly, it has a delicious nutty flavour with chewy texture. You can also buy wholegrain farro which is higher in fibre, but it needs soaking overnight before cooking.

If you can't find farro, you can replace it with pearl (or pearled) barley, which has the same amount of protein, close to the same amount of fibre and is usually quite easy to find. Look in the homebrew section of your supermarket, if it's not in the pasta and rice area, as it's also used for that popular pursuit.

SERVES 1

125 g (4½ oz) pearled farro (spelt)

1 Lebanese (short) cucumber, chopped

100 g (3½ oz) baby rocket (arugula)

1 spring onion (scallion), sliced

½ cup cooked chickpeas (see page 78)

40 g (1½ oz/¼ cup) kalamata olives

100 g (3½ oz) cherry tomatoes, quartered

½ bunch of flat-leaf (Italian) parsley, roughly chopped

100 g (3½ oz) feta cheese, crumbled

DRESSING

3 tablespoons lemon juice

80 ml (2½ fl oz/⅓ cup) olive oil

1 teaspoon dried oregano

2 teaspoons honey

To make the dressing, combine all of the ingredients in a small bowl, season with salt and pepper and whisk to combine. Set aside.

Rinse the farro and put it in a medium saucepan, then add 625 ml (21½ fl oz/2½ cups) of salted water. Bring to a rolling boil, then reduce the heat and simmer, covered, stirring occasionally for 15–20 minutes or until the farro is tender, but still has a little bite left.

Drain the farro, drizzle with a little of the dressing and set aside.

In a medium serving bowl, combine the cucumber, rocket, spring onion, chickpeas, olives, tomatoes and parsley. Add the farro and pour the remaining dressing over.

Scatter the feta over the top and serve.

Tuna, cannellini beans and red onion salad

A superfast store-cupboard lunch filled with protein, prebiotic cannellini beans, brain-boosting fish oils and antioxidants, all topped with a good dose of olive oil.

SERVES 1

95 g (3¼ oz) tin tuna in olive oil

½ cup cooked cannellini beans (tinned beans, rinsed and drained)

½ small red (Spanish) onion, very thinly sliced (use a mandolin if you have one)

4 cherry tomatoes, halved or quartered

handful of flat-leaf (Italian) parsley, roughly chopped

60 ml (2 fl oz/¼ cup) olive oil

juice of ½ lemon

handful of rocket (arugula) leaves

freshly ground black pepper

Combine all of the ingredients in a large bowl, adding pepper to taste. Eat straight away, perhaps with some crusty bread to mop up the lemony juices.

Spiced lamb cutlets with lemony chickpea and tomato salad

Bursting with lamb and chickpea protein as well as plenty of fibre, antioxidants from cumin, turmeric, sesame seeds, and all that lovely salad, this meal is absolutely delicious!

SERVES 2

1 egg

2 teaspoons ground cumin

1 teaspoon turmeric

2 tablespoons sesame seeds

1 teaspoon pepper

4 lamb cutlets

2 tablespoons olive oil, plus 2 tablespoons extra

100 g (3½ oz) cooked chickpeas (see page 78)

200 g (7 oz) cherry tomatoes, halved

1 Lebanese (short) cucumber, chopped

80 g (2¾ oz) mixed salad leaves

½ bunch of flat-leaf (Italian) parsley, chopped

juice and zest of 1 lemon

Lightly beat the egg in a shallow bowl. In a separate shallow bowl, combine the spices and seeds. Bash the cutlets with a rolling pin or meat hammer so they're nice and thin. Dip a cutlet in the egg so both sides are coated, then dip both sides into the spice mix. Place on a baking tray and repeat with the remaining cutlets.

Heat the olive oil in a frying pan over medium heat. Cook the cutlets for 2 minutes each side for medium or until cooked to your liking. Set aside in a warm place while you assemble the salad.

In a large bowl, combine the chickpeas, tomatoes, cucumber, salad leaves, parsley and lemon zest. Pour on the lemon juice and extra olive oil and toss well to combine. Serve with the cutlets.

Stir-fried tofu with sticky peanuts

We're going to pack as many vegetables as we can into one wok! The tofu adds protein and some extra minerals. Tofu is made from soy milk that is treated with a substance such as calcium carbonate, causing it to form curds; it's much like what happens when making cheese from milk. Serve this with a little rice or some noodles if you're extra hungry.

SERVES 2

40 g (1½ oz) peanuts

1 tablespoon refined granulated sugar

1 tablespoon sesame seeds

pinch of chilli powder

2 tablespoons rice bran oil

150 g (5½ oz) firm tofu, cut into cubes

thumb-size piece of fresh ginger, cut into matchsticks

2 garlic cloves, finely chopped

½ bunch of spring onions (scallions), thinly sliced, plus extra to serve

1 carrot, cut into matchsticks

20 g (¾ oz) snow peas (mangetout), thinly sliced diagonally

50 g (1¾ oz) mushrooms, thinly sliced

6 baby corn

2 tablespoons soy sauce

2 tablespoons sesame oil

80 g (2¾ oz/1¾ cups) baby spinach leaves

Mix the peanuts, sugar, sesame seeds and chilli powder with 1 tablespoon of water and a pinch of salt and cook in a wok over medium heat for about 2 minutes until the nuts become sticky and start to caramelise. Scrape on to a plate and set aside to cool.

Wipe out the wok, and reheat over high heat. Add the rice bran oil then toss in the tofu. Stir the tofu around the wok for 2–3 minutes, shaking the wok as you go, until the tofu starts to turn golden. Add the ginger, garlic and spring onion and cook for 2 minutes, then add the carrot, snow peas, mushrooms and baby corn and continue to toss and stir. Add the soy sauce and sesame oil: toss well and then let it sizzle for a moment or two. Add the baby spinach leaves and toss until they start to wilt.

Remove the wok from the heat and immediately divide the stir-fry between two serving bowls, then top with the sticky peanuts and extra spring onion.

Turmeric chicken breast with pumpkin and broccoli

A fast weeknight dinner, lemony chicken with vegetables cooked in the pan juices is stained a golden yellow from that fabulous turmeric, all easily cooked in the one baking dish. You could substitute or add other vegetables depending on what you have on hand: swede (rutabaga), cauliflower, parsnip, sweet potato or carrots would all go well.

SERVES 4

1 tablespoon ground turmeric

1 tablespoon ground ginger

2 garlic cloves, crushed

juice of 1 lemon

2 spring onions (scallions), finely sliced

60 ml (2 fl oz/¼ cup) olive oil

2 large boneless chicken breasts, skin on

½ butternut pumpkin (squash), peeled and cut into small cubes

1 small broccoli, broken into florets

100 g (3½ oz) baby rocket (arugula) leaves

½ bunch of coriander (cilantro) leaves, chopped

Preheat the oven to 200°C (400°F).

In a bowl, combine the turmeric, ginger, garlic, lemon juice and spring onion with the olive oil. Put the chicken into a baking dish, then pour on the turmeric mixture and rub over the chicken. Scatter the pumpkin around the chicken and coat with the dressing.

Roast for 15 minutes. Remove from the oven, turn over the pumpkin and chicken and add the broccoli. Return to the oven and roast for another 15 minutes.

Remove from the oven and cut each chicken breast into thick slices. Divide the rocket between four serving plates, top with the chicken, pumpkin and broccoli and pour on any juices from the baking dish. Scatter with the chopped coriander and serve.

Three-cheese omelette with herbs

You'll need a really good non-stick pan to make a great omelette; however, even in the worst-case scenario, if it doesn't glide effortlessly off the pan, you've got scrambled eggs with cheese.

SERVES 1

3 eggs

2 teaspoons chopped chives

15 g (½ oz) butter, for frying

2 tablespoons grated Gruyere cheese

2 tablespoons soft cheese, such as ricotta or feta

1 tablespoon grated parmesan

salad, to serve

Crack the eggs into a small bowl, add a tablespoon of water and whisk with a fork. Add half of the chopped chives.

Gently heat the butter in a medium non-stick frying pan over medium–low heat until melted and a few bubbles start to appear. Swirl the pan to coat the surface. Pour the egg mixture into the pan. Cook, without stirring, for 10–20 seconds until the egg just starts to set around the edge of the pan. Using a heatproof spatula, stir the egg to start scrambling. When the egg begins to form small loose curds, stop stirring and shake the pan so the eggs form an even layer on the bottom of the pan. Sprinkle the cheeses down the centre of the omelette, in line with the handle. Leave to heat for a few moments: you want the middle to still be soft, and it will continue to cook after you remove it from the heat.

Tilt the pan away from you, still over medium–low heat and, starting with the edge nearest to you, use the spatula to roll the omelette away from you. Keep nudging the omelette until you have rolled it into a neat roll. Slide onto a plate and scatter with the remaining chives. Serve with a lovely big salad.

Pepper minute steak sandwich

Steak is packed with iron and protein, and blue cheese also has high-quality protein and some good strains of probiotics. Balance that with salad in the sandwich. Best of all, it tastes delicious.

SERVES 1

1 minute steak, around 100 g (3½ oz) is plenty

2 sourdough bread slices

1 tablespoon mayonnaise (see page 83)

3–4 small cos (romaine) lettuce leaves

3 tomato slices

2 tablespoons blue cheese, crumbled

Season both sides of the steak with salt and generously with freshly ground black pepper. Heat a heavy-based frying pan over high heat, add the steak and cook for about 1 minute on each side until golden. Remove from the heat and let it rest, and keep warm while you make the toast.

Toast the sourdough bread, then smear one slice with mayonnaise. Add the cos leaves and sliced tomato, then carefully top with the steak and scatter the blue cheese on top. Place the second slice of toast on top of the stack and serve immediately.

Pan-fried fish with butter, peas, leek, lemon and almonds

Butter, lemon juice, fish. This dish just goes to show that simple meals can be a perfect combination of good for you and so delicious.

SERVES 1

generous knob of butter, for frying

1 tablespoon olive oil

1 small leek, white part only, thinly sliced

75 g (2¾ oz/½ cup) peas, fresh or frozen

1 firm white-fleshed fish fillet, such as King George whiting, silver perch or flathead

1 teaspoon ground turmeric

juice of 1 lemon

2 tablespoons slivered almonds, toasted

mixed salad leaves, to serve

In a large frying pan, melt the butter with the olive oil, add the leek and fry gently over medium heat for about 10 minutes until softened. Add the peas and heat through. Remove the leek and peas from the pan, set side and keep warm.

Pat dry the fish fillet with paper towel, sprinkle each side with a little salt and rub in the turmeric.

Add some more butter to the frying pan and heat until it starts to sizzle and smell nutty, then add the fish and cook for 2 minutes or until golden brown. Flip the fish over and cook the other side, spooning butter over the fillet as you go. Return the leek and the peas to the pan with the fish to heat through. Add the lemon juice and remove from the heat.

To serve, place the fish fillet on a plate with the vegetables and any pan juices. Top with the toasted almonds. Serve with mixed salad leaves.

Smashed avocado and peas with goat's cheese

Here's another superfast and super-delicious meal with protein, good fats and antioxidants. You can increase the protein content by adding a poached egg, a slice of bacon or a slice of smoked salmon — all would be delicious. Good vegetarian options would be adding chopped walnuts, some LSA or a handful of savoury granola (see page 81).

SERVES 1

75 g (2¾ oz/½ cup) frozen peas

250 ml (9 fl oz/1 cup) boiling water

½ avocado

2 tablespoons olive oil, plus extra for drizzling

juice of ½ lemon

handful of mint leaves, chopped

1 wholegrain sourdough bread slice, toasted

pinch of turmeric

salt flakes and freshly ground black pepper

20 g (¾ oz) goat's cheese, crumbled

Put the frozen peas in a bowl and pour in the boiling water. Stand for 5 minutes then drain well. Dry the bowl and return the peas. Add the avocado, olive oil, lemon juice and mint and smash and mix with a fork. You don't want a smooth paste by any means, just chunks of smashed peas and avocado.

Place the toast on a plate, moisten with a little olive oil, then tumble the green smash on. Add turmeric, salt and pepper, then crumble the cheese over the top. A little extra drizzle of olive oil won't go astray.

Power porridge

Use traditional rolled (porridge) oats instead of quick oats if you can; they give a better texture to this high-fibre dish. Soak the oats in water overnight, which makes for a creamier porridge in the morning. The porridge can also be made using full-cream milk: this adds extra protein, kilojoules (calories) and calcium to each mouthful and is especially beneficial for anyone who has unintentionally lost some weight or is experiencing reduced appetite.

SERVES 1

PORRIDGE

50 g (1¾ oz/½ cup) rolled (porridge) oats

375 ml (13 fl oz/1½ cups) water

pinch of salt

cream or milk to serve

WINTER PORRIDGE TOPPING

2 teaspoons LSA

½ banana

2 tablespoons chopped pecans

½ teaspoon cinnamon or sweet dukkah (see page 80)

1 tablespoon golden syrup or maple syrup

SUMMER PORRIDGE TOPPING

2 teaspoons LSA

1 teaspoon poppy seeds

80 g (2¾ oz/½ cup) fresh blueberries

handful of toasted hazelnuts (filberts)

2–3 tablespoons coconut flakes

1 tablespoon yoghurt

1 tablespoon honey

In a small saucepan over high heat, combine the oats, water and salt and bring to the boil, stirring occasionally. Reduce the heat to low and simmer, stirring gently and constantly for up to 8 minutes. Don't let anything stick to the bottom of the pan.

When you pour it into a serving bowl, let it set for a minute or so. Add a splash of cream or milk: if the finished porridge spins in the milk you win! Try the topping ideas below.

Winter porridge

Make the porridge as above and stir in the LSA before pouring into the bowl. Top with the banana and pecans, then sprinkle the cinnamon on top and drizzle with syrup. Serve at once.

Summer porridge

Make the basic porridge recipe as above, then stir in the LSA and poppy seeds. Pour into a bowl and top with the blueberries and hazelnuts, then finish with yoghurt and drizzle of honey.

fast SALADS

No longer restricted to the side of the plate, these show-stopping salads take centre stage, filled with colours, textures and flavours that your brain and your tastebuds will applaud.

Red cabbage, pea, mint and feta salad with poppy seeds

Frozen peas are little different nutritionally to fresh, providing protein and prebiotic fibre. So, unless you happen to have a vegie patch out the back, keep frozen peas in your freezer. Feta and poppy seeds add to the protein in this dish and add to the brain-boosting antioxidants from the cabbage and mint. This salad keeps really well, so you can make a double serve and store the leftovers in an airtight container in the fridge.

SERVES 2

75 g (2¾ oz/½ cup) frozen peas

boiling water, to cover

¼ red cabbage

handful of chopped mint

50 g (1¾ oz) feta cheese, crumbled

2 tablespoons poppy seeds

2 tablespoons macadamia oil or olive oil

juice of 1 lemon

Put the peas in a heatproof bowl and cover with boiling water. Stand for 5 minutes to defrost, then drain: you don't want to cook them, just bring them to room temperature. Meanwhile, thinly slice the cabbage (on a mandolin if you dare) and put it in a large bowl, then add the drained peas. Add the remaining ingredients and toss well to combine. Season with salt and pepper as desired, and serve.

Winter caesar salad with walnuts

What a great winter salad this makes! It mixes the prebiotic benefits of cabbage with protein and omega-3 from anchovies and walnuts — all easy to get hold of through winter when the vegie garden is having a rest. Thinly shaved Brussels sprouts are a delicious addition to the cabbage in this salad when they are in season.

SERVES 2-3

2 bacon rashers

olive oil, for frying

75 g (2¾ oz/1 cup) shaved white cabbage or Brussels sprouts

¼ purple cabbage

1 large carrot, peeled

80 ml (2½ fl oz/⅓ cup) lemon juice

2 anchovies, finely chopped

2 tablespoons dijon mustard

80 ml (2½ fl oz/⅓ cup) olive oil

30 g (1 oz/¼ cup) walnuts, toasted

35 g (1¼ oz/⅓ cup) finely grated parmesan cheese

Use a sharp knife to cut the bacon into 1 cm (⅜ inch) strips, make sure you leave on all of the fat. Heat a small heavy-based frying pan over medium heat and add a splash of olive oil. Cook the bacon slices gently over medium–low heat for about 15 minutes, stirring occasionally, until the bacon is golden and crispy, then set aside.

Shave the white cabbage or Brussels sprouts and purple cabbage into fine shreds using a mandolin, or cut into thin-as-you-can slices with a sharp knife. Transfer to a large bowl. Slice the carrots into thin coins and add to the cabbage mixture.

Combine the lemon juice, anchovies, mustard and olive oil in a small bowl and whisk with a fork to emulsify into a dressing. Season with salt and pepper. Taste the dressing: if it's too tart, add a bit more olive oil and if it's not sharp enough, add a bit more mustard or lemon juice.

Add the walnuts to the cabbage mixture and pour the dressing over the top. Toss until all of the vegetables are lightly coated in the dressing. Sprinkle half of the parmesan over the salad and toss again, then add the remaining parmesan and the bacon and toss again.

Roast beetroot with feta, walnuts and dill

Beetroot packs an anthocyanin (a type of antioxidant) punch and it looks so good in this salad too. Walnuts are added for omega-3, feta for protein and calcium, and all those greens are topped off with gorgeous olive oil. What could be better!

SERVES 2 AS A MEAL OR 4 AS A SIDE DISH

6 baby beetroot (beets)

2 tablespoons olive oil, plus 2 tablespoons extra

1 teaspoon salt

zest and juice of 1 orange

100 (3½ oz) mixed green salad leaves

80 (2¾ oz) feta cheese, crumbled

60 g (2¼ oz/½ cup) walnuts, toasted

Preheat the oven to 200°C (400°F).

Rub each beetroot with olive oil and sprinkle with salt. Put them in a baking tray and add a tablespoon of water. Cover with foil and roast for 30–40 minutes until tender. The roasting time depends on the size of the beetroot; pierce with a sharp knife to test whether they are soft. Remove from the oven and set aside to cool. You can store them in the fridge for up to 4 days.

When cool enough to handle, peel the beetroot and cut into wedges (wear rubber gloves if you don't want to stain your hands) then add to a salad bowl.

Add the remaining ingredients except the feta and walnuts and toss well to combine. Pour onto a serving platter and scatter the feta and walnuts over the top to serve.

New Waldorf salad

You're not going to use all of the celery, but you need to buy at least a half bunch so you get the pale, tasty heart. Store leftover celery in the crisper of the fridge. Delicious, crisp and packed with good fats from the oil, nuts and mayonnaise.

SERVES 2

1 apple, cored and sliced

juice of 1 lemon

½ bunch of celery, especially the heart

handful of green salad leaves

a few leaves of radicchio

60 g (2¼ oz/½ cup) walnuts, toasted

2 tablespoons walnut oil, or olive oil

2 tablespoons mayonnaise (see page 83)

rye bread slice, to serve (optional)

Put the apple slices in a salad bowl and sprinkle with lemon juice. Toss to coat so the slices don't go brown.

Tear out the heart of the celery and finely chop into 1 cm (⅜ inch) pieces, including the pale leaves. You'll need about a cupful of celery but you can add an extra stalk or two if you're feeling hungry. Add the chopped celery to the apple. Add the green salad leaves, radicchio and walnuts and drizzle the walnut oil over the top. Season with salt and pepper.

To serve, pile the salad onto a plate and top with a generous dollop of mayonnaise. You can serve the salad on a slice of dark rye bread, but it's pretty filling without.

Avocado Caprese salad

Avocado is such a creamy, delicious source of good fats; when you add a bit of protein from pine nuts and bocconcini and plenty of antioxidants from rocket, tomatoes, garlic and basil, this salad makes a hit.

SERVES 2

40 g (1½ oz/¼ cup) pine nuts

150 g (5½ oz) rocket (arugula) leaves

1 avocado

250 g (9 oz) cherry tomatoes

150 g–200 g (5½ oz–7 oz) bocconcini

7 g (¼ oz/¼ cup) fresh basil leaves

DRESSING

1 garlic clove, crushed

¼ teaspoon salt

1 teaspoon sugar

1 teaspoon balsamic vinegar

60 ml (2 fl oz/¼ cup) olive oil

Put the pine nuts in a dry frying pan and cook over medium–low heat, stirring frequently, until golden brown, about 2 minutes. Remove from the heat and transfer them to a cool plate to stop the cooking process. Set aside.

To make the salad, toss the rocket leaves into a large salad bowl. Peel the avocado and discard the stone; chop the avocado flesh and toss over the rocket leaves. Halve the cherry tomatoes and add to the rocket and avocado. Tear the bocconcini in halves and toss them into the bowl.

Roll most of the basil leaves up into a tight bundle and thinly slice, then scatter over the salad, along with the remaining whole leaves.

To make the salad dressing, put the garlic into a small bowl, add the salt, sugar, balsamic vinegar and olive oil and whisk well to combine. Pour the dressing over the salad.

Top with toasted pine nuts and serve. You can also add cooked chicken pieces to increase the protein content of this salad.

Chargrilled broccoli mimosa

Beautiful and full of antioxidants and prebiotic, anti-inflammatory goodness, broccoli combines so well with olive oil and apple cider vinegar, while the egg and pumpkin seeds top it all off with a protein boost.

SERVES 2

1 tablespoon apple cider vinegar

2 teaspoons dijon mustard

60 ml (2 fl oz/¼ cup) olive oil, plus extra for frying

1 small broccoli

1 hard-boiled egg, peeled

handful of pumpkin seeds (pepitas)

colourful salad leaves, to serve

To make a vinaigrette, whisk together the vinegar, mustard and olive oil, season with salt and pepper as desired, then set aside.

Peel the broccoli stem of any thick woody skin. Then cut the broccoli lengthways so you have long stems with the florets on the end. Each floret should be about 3 cm wide, so they cook quickly and evenly.

Heat a chargrill pan over medium–high heat, add a splash of olive oil then add the broccoli spears. Turn down the heat to medium and cook until the broccoli starts to turn golden, turning occasionally so that each side is cooked.

Remove the broccoli from the heat and place on a serving plate. Pour the vinaigrette over. Hold a coarse sieve over the broccoli, and push the boiled egg through the sieve so that it falls over the broccoli in a pretty, fluffy garnish. Scatter the pumpkin seeds over and serve at once with a side salad of colourful leaves.

Avocado, grapefruit, green bean and hazelnut salad

Avocado is so irresistible: this time combining the crunch and zing of lettuce and apple cider vinegar with hazelnuts for protein and antioxidants, and lovely olive oil to top off the good fats.

SERVES 2

200 g (7 oz) green beans, washed and trimmed

1 grapefruit, ruby or pink if you can get it

1 baby cos (romaine) lettuce, torn

1 avocado, sliced

50 g (1¾ oz/⅓ cup) hazelnuts (filberts), toasted and skin removed

2 tablespoons olive oil

1 tablespoon apple cider vinegar

In a large saucepan of salted boiling water, cook the beans for 3–8 minutes until tender.

Drain and transfer the beans to a large bowl of iced water, to stop further cooking. Stand for 5 minutes, then drain, pat dry and set aside.

Over a small bowl, use a sharp knife to cut the skin and any white pith from the grapefruit and then cut into segments, letting any juice collect in the bowl. Reserve the juice.

Divide the lettuce between two wide shallow bowls and top with the avocado slices and beans. Finish with the grapefruit segments then scatter the hazelnuts over.

Drizzle with 1–2 tablespoons of the reserved grapefruit juice, then the olive oil and vinegar.

Season to taste with salt and pepper as desired, and serve.

Chargrilled corn, zucchini and tomato salad with nuts

Blending the colour and antioxidants of the corn, zucchini, tomatoes and coriander (cilantro) with the protein of black beans and tahini and the prebiotic fibre of beans and corn. A body and brain treat!

SERVES 4 AS A SIDE DISH

3 sweetcorn cobs, husks and silk removed

1 zucchini (courgette)

70 g (2½ oz/½ cup) cherry tomatoes

½ bunch of coriander (cilantro), leaves and stems

2 spring onions (scallions)

110 g (3¾ oz/½ cup) black beans, cooked (see page 77)

60 g (2¼ oz/½ cup) walnuts, toasted and chopped

1 avocado

1 fresh red chilli, seeds removed and sliced

CREAMY TAHINI LIME DRESSING

3 tablespoons tahini

60 ml (2 fl oz/¼ cup) lime juice (from 1–2 limes, depending on how juicy they are)

1 teaspoon maple syrup

1 teaspoon sesame oil

1 garlic clove, crushed

pinch of chilli powder

Preheat a barbecue or chargrill pan to hot and grill the corn until it starts to turn a golden colour, turning several times to get a nice even charring.

When the corn is cool enough to handle, put the tip into a bowl and hold the stalk with your fingers. Use a sharp knife to cut the kernels off the cob and into the bowl. Discard the cob and set aside the kernels.

Finely chop the zucchini into pieces about the same size as the corn kernels. Add this to the corn. Halve the cherry tomatoes, finely chop the coriander and spring onion and add those to the bowl along with the black beans and walnuts. Halve and slice the avocado and gently place the slices around the top of the salad. Finish with the chilli slices.

To make the dressing, mix all of the ingredients in a small bowl and whisk together until well combined. Season with salt and pepper if needed. Add some water, a tablespoon at a time, until you get a thin pouring consistency, like cream.

Drizzle it over the salad and boom!

Lentil tabouleh with goat's cheese

There is so much nutritional good going for this recipe, it's hard to know where to start: swapping the traditional burghul (bulgur) for lentils makes this salad a protein-rich meal. Combine that with plenty of colour, fibre and goodness from the herbs and this is a brain treat! If you're really hungry, add some grilled chicken breasts that have been marinated in lemon juice, garlic and olive oil.

SERVES 4

200 g (7 oz) French green lentils

150 g (5½ oz) cherry tomatoes, quartered

½ bunch of flat-leaf (Italian) parsley, finely chopped

½ bunch of dill, finely chopped

3 spring onions (scallions), finely sliced

2 Lebanese (short) cucumbers, halved lengthways and sliced

2 tablespoons olive oil

juice of 1 lemon

red leaf lettuce, such as mizuna or red oak leaf, to serve

100 g (3½ oz) goat's curd or soft goat's cheese

50 g (1¾ oz) almonds, roughly chopped

In a medium saucepan, cover the lentils with 500 ml (17 fl oz/2 cups) of cold water and a teaspoon of salt, if desired. Bring to the boil, then reduce the heat and simmer until tender. Drain the lentils and spread them out on a tray to cool.

In a large bowl, combine the cooled lentils, tomatoes, parsley, dill, spring onion and cucumbers. Add the olive oil and lemon juice and season with salt. Taste for seasoning: you want a nice salty tang. Add more lemon juice and salt if needed.

Divide the red lettuce leaves equally among four plates, add a generous mound of the tabouleh and top with goat's curd and a scattering of almonds.

MORE
substantial
MEALS

We've given a few classic dinner favourites a healthy brain makeover, plus there are a few delicious new ideas for meals when you're looking for something more sustaining.

Slow-cooked turmeric and ginger lamb ribs

Sticky lamb ribs loaded with turmeric and ginger, served on rice with lots of steamed broccolini on the side. The protein and easily absorbed iron and zinc in all meals using red meats are a benefit. Iron deficiency is not uncommon in older people who are not eating well, and as iron is needed for brain cells to use oxygen for everything they need to do, we need to come up with ways to avoid that. You don't necessarily have to eat red meat every day, but enjoying meals like this one now and then helps. The addition of turmeric, sesame oil and garlic, balanced with a big serve of fresh green vegetables gives this dish anti-inflammatory and prebiotic benefits too.

TIP: You can substitute pork or beef ribs if lamb ribs aren't available.

SERVES 4

500 g (1 lb 2 oz) lamb ribs

thumb-size piece of ginger, sliced

thumb-size piece of turmeric, sliced (or use 1 tablespoon ground)

4 garlic cloves, chopped

2 tablespoons golden syrup (light treacle) or brown sugar

60 ml (2 fl oz/¼ cup) soy sauce

2 tablespoons sesame oil

½ teaspoon salt

1 teaspoon pepper

TO SERVE

spring onion (scallion), sliced

sesame seeds, to serve

steamed rice, to serve

2 bunches of broccolini, steamed (optional)

Preheat the oven to 180°C (350°F).

Put the lamb in a casserole dish with a lid. Mix the ginger, turmeric, garlic, golden syrup, soy sauce, sesame oil, salt and pepper and 2 tablespoons of water together in a small bowl. Pour over the lamb and turn to coat well. Cook in the oven with the lid on for 60 minutes. Remove from oven, give the ribs a stir and return to the oven without the lid for another 30 minutes.

Serve on a bed of steamed rice with broccolini on the side, if using. Scatter with spring onion and sesame seeds and serve.

The new tuna mornay

We've ditched the macaroni for broccoli and cauliflower, and increased the protein content of the traditional breadcrumb topping so this dish is now positively a health food. You're welcome.

SERVES 4

½ cauliflower, broken into florets

½ broccoli, broken into florets

2 tablespoons olive oil

1 teaspoon turmeric

1 teaspoon salt

185 g (6½ oz) tin tuna chunks in oil

mixed salad leaves and tomato wedges, to serve

TOPPING

100 g (3½ oz) wholemeal flour

50 g (1¾ oz) butter, diced

50 g (1¾ oz/½ cup) grated cheddar cheese

25 g (1 oz/¼ cup) rolled (porridge) oats

2 tablespoons LSA

1 teaspoon black pepper

SAUCE

2 tablespoons butter

1 garlic clove, finely chopped

2 tablespoons plain (all-purpose) flour

30 g (1 oz/⅓ cup) grated cheddar cheese

400 ml (14 fl oz) milk

pinch of ground nutmeg

Preheat oven to 200°C (400°F).

Put the cauliflower and broccoli in a 15 x 20 cm (6 x 8 inch) baking dish, drizzle the olive oil over the top and add the turmeric and salt. Toss everything with your hands until it's all well coated. Roast for about 15 minutes or until the cauliflower is starting to turn golden brown.

Meanwhile, to make the topping, put the flour, butter, cheese, oats, LSA and pepper into the bowl of a food processor and pulse until it resembles breadcrumbs. Set aside.

To make the sauce, heat a large saucepan over medium–high heat and melt the butter until it bubbles slightly. Add the garlic and stir for a minute, then add the flour and stir well for another minute. Using a whisk to stir, add the milk a little at a time, whisking constantly. Continue to cook over medium heat, stirring all the time and making sure it doesn't catch on the bottom, until the sauce thickens. Add the cheese and stir until melted and combined. Remove from the heat and season with salt, if desired, and the nutmeg.

Remove the dish of vegetables from the oven and empty the tin of tuna over the top. Break it up a bit so it's evenly distributed. Pour the sauce over.

Spread the topping all over the the vegetables and tuna. You should cover all of them and have a nice thick crumble topping.

Put the dish onto a baking tray (to catch any spills) and return it to the oven to cook until the crumble is golden brown all over.

Allow to cool for 10 minutes before serving with a huge salad.

Whole baked sweet potatoes with yoghurt, chickpea and tomato salad

Baked sweet potatoes are a delicious alternative to regular potatoes and they also pack in the antioxidants. You can always fill them with old favourites such as sour cream, herbs and crispy bacon or the beans on page 99. Or try this brainy alternative.

SERVES 4

4 small sweet potatoes

200 g (7 oz/1 cup) chickpeas, cooked (see page 78)

2 large tomatoes, finely chopped

handful of baby rocket (arugula) leaves

2 tablespoons olive oil

50 g (1¾ oz/½ cup) grated cheddar cheese

95 g (3¼ oz/⅓ cup) yoghurt

55 g (1¾ oz/⅓ cup) toasted pumpkin seeds (pepitas)

Preheat the oven to 200°C (400°F). Use a fork to pierce each sweet potato several times all over. Put the sweet potatoes on a baking tray lined with baking paper.

Bake the sweet potatoes about 1 hour until tender. To check if they're cooked, test with a small knife.

To make the salad, use the back of a spoon to crush the chickpeas until they are a little broken up so they don't roll everywhere, but not a smooth paste. Add the tomato, rocket leaves, olive oil and season with salt and pepper.

Use a small, sharp knife to make a slit along the top of each sweet potato. Gently squeeze the potato to open it up, add the cheese then fill with salad and top with yoghurt and pumpkin seeds.

Burrito-style chicken bowl

So fresh and crunchy, tangy chicken tops a bowl full of colourful vegetables for an antioxidant-packed bowl of brain goodness.

SERVES 2

2 chicken breast fillets

juice of ½ lime

60 ml (2 fl oz/¼ cup) olive oil

1 teaspoon ground turmeric

1 teaspoon ground coriander

½ teaspoon cayenne pepper

220 g (7¾ oz/1 cup) black beans, cooked (see page 77)

1 large tomato, finely chopped

kernels from 1 corncob

1 avocado, halved

1 baby cos (romaine) lettuce

65 g (2½ oz/¼ cup) sour cream, to serve

2 spring onions (scallions), finely chopped, to serve

small bunch of coriander (cilantro) leaves, to serve

1 fresh red chilli, seeds removed, sliced, to serve (optional)

lime halves, to serve

In a medium bowl, mix the chicken breast with the lime juice, olive oil and spices. Cover the chicken and allow to marinate in the fridge for 15 minutes or up to 3 days.

Heat a barbecue, chargrill pan or frying pan to medium–high heat, lay the chicken on the grill and cook for 5 minutes on each side until golden. Transfer to a warm plate and set aside.

Arrange the beans and vegetables in sections around two bowls. Slice the chicken breasts diagonally and place on top. Finish with a spoonful of sour cream and chopped spring onion, coriander leaves and chilli (if using). Serve with lime halves.

Pork sausage with green colcannon

Sausages might not be your first thought when it comes to brain food, but if you get quality ones, and they are not only inexpensive compared with many meat cuts, but they are a way to boost food sustainability by using meat that can't be sold as steak or in larger pieces. And because they come from meat, they still provide protein and minerals such as iron and zinc. In this recipe that's all balanced with the prebiotic fibre from potatoes, cabbage, onions and kale. Bangers and mash get a makeover. If you can't find good-quality pork sausage, beef or lamb might be a better option. A visit to the local butcher might be your best bet.

SERVES 4

4 large potatoes, scrubbed

200 ml (7 fl oz) milk, for mashing

50 g (1¾ oz) butter, for mashing

1 tablespoon olive oil, plus extra for frying sausages

4 100% pork sausages

1 tablespoon butter, plus extra to serve

¼ green cabbage, finely chopped

50 g (1¾ oz/2 cups) kale leaves (stalks removed, sliced)

4 spring onions (scallions), finely sliced

buttered carrots (see facing page), to serve

mustard, to serve

Cook the potatoes in plenty of salted water. Drain and roughly mash with the milk and butter, and season with salt and pepper. Heat a medium frying pan over medium heat, drizzle with a little oil and add the sausages and cook, turning regularly until brown on all sides.

In a large frying pan, heat the olive oil and butter and cook the cabbage and kale over medium heat until soft and wilted. Combine the cabbage mixture with the mashed potatoes and mix through, then add the spring onion.

To serve, spoon the colcannon onto a plate, then make a small dip in the top with a spoon and add a little butter to melt into a golden puddle. Add the sausages and the carrots and serve with buttered carrots and mustard.

BUTTERED CARROTS

300 g (10½ oz) carrots, peeled and sliced diagonally	
30 g (1 oz) butter	
1 tablespoon brown sugar	
½ teaspoon dill seeds	

TO MAKE THE BUTTERED CARROTS

Cook the carrots in a large saucepan of boiling water until tender. Drain. Set the carrots aside. Stir the butter, brown sugar and dill seeds into the pan. Heat gently until the butter melts. Return the carrots to the pan and toss to coat. Cover, and stand for a few minutes to allow the flavours to mingle.

Pumpkin, miso and bean stew

This is a humble Japanese-inspired recipe that is so simple and makes a delicious midwinter dish. Who can go past the flavour, colour and all-round nurturing feel of pumpkin, especially in the cooler months? Add the kidney beans to supply all those great things common to all the pulses: probiotic fibre, protein and antioxidants. If you can find adzuki beans, they offer a distinctly 'Japanese' sensation to this gorgeous dish. The seaweed is an important supplier of a number of nutrients, particularly iodine: a vital nutrient for brain health that is often in short supply in most Western diets.

SERVES 4

220 g (7¾ oz/1 cup) red kidney beans or adzuki beans, soaked overnight

2 tablespoons olive oil

1 tablespoon butter

1 red (Spanish) onion

4–5 garlic cloves, finely chopped

thumb-size piece of ginger, finely grated

1 kg (2 lb 4 oz) pumpkin (winter squash) or butternut pumpkin (squash), peeled and cut into small chunks

1 nori sheet, torn

2 tablespoons miso paste

60 ml (2 fl oz/¼ cup) apple cider vinegar

2 teaspoons tamari (gluten-free soy sauce) or light soy sauce

2 tablespoons sesame seeds, toasted

2 spring onions (scallions), thinly sliced

Cook the beans with plenty of water in a large saucepan over medium–high heat until soft. Drain and set aside.

In a large Dutch oven or flameproof casserole dish, heat the olive oil and butter over medium heat and fry the onion, garlic and grated ginger until fragrant. Add the pumpkin and seaweed and stir for about 5 minutes until the pumpkin is starting to colour. Add the beans, cover with 500 ml (17 fl oz/2 cups) of water, and reduce the heat so the stew gently simmers. In a small bowl, mix the miso, cider vinegar and soy sauce to a smooth paste. Add to the pumpkin mixture and stir. Cook for about 30 minutes or until the pumpkin is tender. Serve in bowls scattered with the sesame seeds and spring onion.

Corned beef with mustard sauce and braised red cabbage

Here is a delicious update to this favourite comfort food: the lean beef packs in the protein and minerals, and the spices and vegetables add the antioxidants and colour. This recipe will make enough corned beef for leftovers the next day. Store it in the fridge for up to four days.

SERVES 4

1.5 kg (3 lb 5 oz) piece of corned beef

½ teaspoon cloves

1 teaspoon grated nutmeg

1 tablespoon black peppercorns

45 g (1½ oz/¼ cup lightly packed) brown sugar, plus 60 g (2¼ oz/ ⅓ cup lightly packed) extra

125 ml (4 fl oz/½ cup) apple cider vinegar

6 potatoes, peeled

4 carrots, peeled

½ small red cabbage, finely sliced

1 small apple, sliced

½ red (Spanish) onion, sliced

½ teaspoon salt

50 g (1¾ oz) butter

125 ml (4 fl oz/½ cup) vinegar

MUSTARD SAUCE

1 tablespoon butter

1 tablespoon plain (all-purpose) flour

1½ tablespoons mustard powder

300 ml (10½ fl oz) milk, warmed

10 g (½ oz/½ cup) flat-leaf (Italian) parsley, chopped

Put the beef in a large saucepan, then add the spices, brown sugar and vinegar. Add enough water to generously cover the beef, then bring to the boil over high heat. Reduce to a simmer and cook for 1 hour. Add the potatoes and carrots, then simmer for another hour or until tender.

Meanwhile, put half of the cabbage, apple and onion in a medium saucepan and cover with the extra brown sugar. Add the remaining cabbage, apple and onion. Add the salt, butter and vinegar, then cover with a lid and cook over very low heat for about 1½ hours.

To make the mustard sauce, melt the butter in a small saucepan. Add the flour and mustard powder and cook for about 1 minute to make a paste. Gradually stir in the milk and continue to stir constantly, until the sauce boils and thickens. Season with salt and freshly ground black pepper, then add the chopped parsley.

To serve, remove the beef from the stock and thickly slice. Serve with the braised cabbage, potatoes and carrots, then pour the mustard sauce over.

Lamb kofta lettuce wraps

Juicy spiced parcels of protein, antioxidants and anti-inflammatory goodness that use lettuce instead of bread. Adding yoghurt, nuts and fresh herbs makes this Mediterranean-inspired dish tick all the nutritional boxes.

SERVES 4

400 g (14 oz) minced (ground) lamb

2 teaspoons ground coriander

1 teaspoon ground cumin

1 teaspoon ground cinnamon

1 teaspoon salt

2 garlic cloves, finely chopped

1 teaspoon lemon zest

1 tablespoon dried mint

olive oil, for frying kofta

260 g (9¼ oz/1 cup) Greek-style yoghurt

8 large cos (romaine) lettuce leaves

SALAD

40 g (1½ oz/¼ cup) hazelnuts (filberts), toasted, skins removed and roughly chopped

65 g (2½ oz/½ cup) crumbled feta cheese

2 large tomatoes, chopped

handful of fresh marjoram, chopped

2 tablespoons lemon juice

2 tablespoons olive oil

Use your hands to knead together the lamb mince and the spices, garlic, lemon zest and mint until really well blended. Divide into eight portions and roll into football-shaped ovals with your hands. Put them on a plate in the fridge while you make the salad.

To make the salad, put all of the ingredients in a small bowl and toss to combine. Season with salt and pepper and set aside.

Heat a barbecue, chargrill pan or frying pan to medium–high heat and smear with a little olive oil. Add the koftas and cook for 3–4 minutes. Don't move them until a crust develops, then turn over and cook each side. Remove from the heat.

To assemble, place a spoonful of yoghurt onto each lettuce leaf, add a spoonful of salad and top with a kofta. Fold the lettuce around the filling and eat.

Fish cakes with rainbow slaw

With the brainpower of omega-3 and vitamin D from the salmon and the addition of quinoa for extra protein, fibre and antioxidants, these fish cakes will do nicely. Add the slaw to this, or any other dish you fancy, and your brain will certainly thank you!

SERVES 4

250 g (9 oz) cooked red quinoa

250 g (9 oz) hot-smoked salmon

1 carrot, grated

2 eggs, beaten

1 tablespoon capers (rinsed if in salt), chopped

zest and juice of 1 lemon

2 tablespoons chopped fresh dill

2 tablespoons chopped chives

oil, for frying

lemon wedges to serve

RAINBOW SLAW

¼ red cabbage, finely sliced

2 carrots, finely sliced or grated

2 radishes, sliced

½ fennel bulb, finely sliced

½ bunch of flat-leaf (Italian) parsley, chopped

juice and zest of ½ lemon

2 tablespoons olive oil

40 g (1½ oz/¼ cup) toasted pumpkin seeds (pepitas)

PAPRIKA MAYONNAISE

½ cup mayonnaise (see page 83)

1 teaspoon smoked paprika

In a large bowl, mix together the quinoa, salmon, carrot, eggs, capers, lemon zest and juice and herbs until really well combined. The mix should feel quite sticky. Cover and refrigerate for 30 minutes. This cooling time makes it easier to form into cakes. Now, form into cakes about 9 cm (3½ inches) in diameter. Place the cakes on a cool baking sheet or plate and refrigerate for another 30 minutes to help them stick together.

In a large frying pan, heat enough oil to coat the bottom of the pan. Fry the cakes in the hot oil, making sure not to crowd them as this reduces the heat and makes for soggy cakes. Cook the cakes until they are very golden brown on both sides, turning carefully to prevent them breaking. When this batch is done pop them onto a baking tray lined with baking paper and into a warm 120°C (250°F) oven. Cook the remaining cakes.

To make the rainbow slaw, toss all the ingredients together and season with salt and pepper.

Stir the paprika into the mayonnaise.

Serve the fish cakes on a plate with the rainbow slaw, mayonnaise and lemon wedges.

smart SOUPS

These soups will nourish your brain and soul. Not only is soup a comfort food, it's a great way to use seasonal produce and pack in all sorts of nutrients. Store leftovers in the freezer to enjoy another day.

Turmeric, pumpkin and sweet potato soup

Straight pumpkin soup might draw a yawn … but add sweet potato and loads of ginger and turmeric, and you get plenty of potassium, antioxidants and anti-inflammatory offerings. Serving it with crispy garlic chips adds a flavour-packed crunch.

SERVES 4

40 g (1½ oz/¼ cup) pumpkin seeds (pepitas)

80 ml (2½ oz/⅓ cup) coconut oil

4 garlic cloves, sliced

300 g (10½ oz) pumpkin (squash), peeled and chopped

300 g (10½ oz) sweet potato, peeled and chopped

½ red (Spanish) onion, finely chopped

1 tablespoon ground turmeric, or 2 tablespoons freshly grated

1 tablespoon freshly grated ginger

½ teaspoon pepper

1 litre (35 fl oz/4 cups) vegetable stock or water

270 ml (9½ fl oz) tin coconut milk

First make the toppings for your soup. Heat a small frying pan over medium heat and dry-fry the pumpkin seeds until they start to colour and pop. Remove from the heat, transfer the seeds to a small bowl and set aside.

Melt 2 tablespoons of the coconut oil in the same frying pan over medium heat, add the garlic, reduce the heat to low and fry the garlic until it just starts to turn golden. Quickly transfer to a plate lined with paper towel and set aside.

In a large heavy-based saucepan, melt the remaining coconut oil and add the chopped vegetables. Cook over medium heat until the onion has softened and the vegetables are starting to colour. Add the turmeric, ginger and pepper, and stir and cook for a few moments. Add the stock, increase the heat and bring to the boil. Reduce the heat to a simmer and cook until the vegetables are completely soft.

Remove from the heat and use a stick blender to purée the vegetables until you have a smooth soup. Return to medium heat, add the coconut milk and cook until just returning to the boil, then reduce the heat and simmer for a few minutes until ready to serve. Season with salt and pepper if desired. (The amount of salt you will need depends on whether you used vegetable stock or water.)

To serve, ladle the soup into bowls and scatter the pumpkin seeds and crispy garlic over the top.

Tofu and miso broth

Simple, nourishing broth that's fast to make and is positively brimming with goodness. All the benefits of soya (in tofu), combined with the prebiotic bonus of buckwheat (in soba noodles) and the myriad benefits of mushrooms, seaweed and sesame.

SERVES 2

160 g (5¾ oz) soba noodles

4–5 tablespoons miso paste

200 g (7 oz) firm tofu, cut into 2 cm (¾ inch) cubes

155 g (5½ oz) carrots, cut into matchsticks

1 cup mushrooms, stalks removed and thinly sliced

2 spring onions (scallions), white and green parts separated, thinly sliced

2 tablespoons sesame seeds, toasted

1 nori sheet, cut into small slivers

sesame oil, to serve

Cook the noodles according to the directions on the packet and set aside.

Fill a medium saucepan with 2 litres (70 fl oz/8 cups) of water and stir through the miso paste over medium–low heat until the miso has dissolved. Add the tofu, carrot, mushrooms and the white part of the spring onion and cook until warmed through.

Divide the noodles between two soup bowls, ladle the broth into the bowls and add the vegetables and tofu. Top with the nori slivers, the green part of the spring onion and the toasted sesame seeds. Drizzle with sesame oil to serve.

Chicken and rosemary soup

You can use any type of kale for this: such as Tuscan kale or red leaf kale (if the leaves are big make sure you remove the tough stalk). Chicken soup is decidedly good for the soul and the addition here of the antioxidant-rich kale and other vegies plus the prebiotic-rich lentils just tops it off.

SERVES 2

generous knob of butter, for frying

1 red (Spanish) onion, finely sliced

2 garlic cloves, chopped

2 celery stalks, finely chopped

50 g (1¾ oz/2 cups) kale leaves (stalks removed, sliced)

2 litres (70 fl oz/8 cups) chicken stock

210 g (7½ oz/1 cup) green lentils, cooked (see page 78)

2 rosemary sprigs, leaves picked

175 g (6 oz/1 cup) shredded cooked chicken meat

freshly ground black pepper, to serve

extra virgin olive oil, to serve

In a large heavy-based saucepan, melt the butter over medium heat then add the onion, garlic, celery and kale, cooking until softened. Add the chicken stock, lentils and rosemary leaves and simmer for 10–15 minutes. Add the cooked chicken and cook until heated through.

Serve with a sprinkle of pepper and a swirl of olive oil.

Oxtail and kidney bean chilli

You'll need to start this recipe a day ahead to soak the kidney beans overnight. Or you can use drained tinned kidney beans, but as they're already cooked, add them right at the end of cooking to just heat through. The beans are a prebiotic powerhouse supporting the gut–brain axis, while slow-cooking the beef actually improves the accessibility of minerals such as iron and zinc. That is all boosted by a beautiful mix of spices and herbs. This is super rich, but the lime and coriander (cilantro) cut through the richness.

SERVES 4

500 g (1 lb 2 oz) oxtail, cut into chunks

1 tablespoon olive oil, plus extra

1 red (Spanish) onion, finely chopped

2 garlic cloves, finely chopped

2 celery stalks, finely chopped

½ red capsicum (pepper), finely chopped

½ bunch of coriander (cilantro)

400 g (14 oz) tin chopped tomatoes

1 teaspoon dried oregano

1 teaspoon ground cumin

1 tablespoon ground coriander

¼ teaspoon cayenne pepper

1 tablespoon ground cinnamon

1 teaspoon dried chilli flakes (more if you like it super spicy)

1 teaspoon black pepper

1 teaspoon salt (or to taste)

185 g (6½ oz/1 cup) dried red kidney beans, soaked in water overnight

crumbled feta and lime wedges, to serve

Season the oxtail with salt and pepper.

In a large, heavy-based flameproof casserole dish or saucepan, heat the olive oil over medium–high heat then add the seasoned oxtail to brown. Remove the oxtail from the pan and set aside. Add a little extra olive oil and the onion, garlic, celery and capsicum and cook over medium heat until the onion has softened. Finely chop the stems from the coriander and add to the saucepan, then add the tomatoes, herbs and spices. Drain the kidney beans and discard the soaking water and add to the pan. Fill the tomato tin with water and pour that in with an extra 1 litre (35 fl oz/4 cups) of water. Return the oxtail to the pan and simmer for about 3 hours, stirring occasionally, or until the oxtail is tender and falling off the bone. Keep an eye on the liquid level, as you may need to add more water.

Scoop the oxtail from the pan and set aside to cool (if you're using tinned kidney beans add them now.) Pick all the meat off the oxtail bones and return the meat to the pan, discarding the bones. Crumble the feta over the top, scatter with coriander leaves and add a squeeze of lime.

Borscht

This is so delicious, nutrient-packed and simple to make, reviving even the most weary.

SERVES 4

1 tablespoon butter

2 cm (¾ inch) thick beef shin (osso bucco), about 400 g (14 oz)

1 large onion, roughly chopped

2 large carrots, roughly chopped

2 celery stalks with leaves, roughly chopped

2 bay leaves

60 ml (2 fl oz/¼ cup) apple cider vinegar

3 large beetroot (beets), peeled and chopped

¼ red cabbage, finely sliced

TO SERVE

2 hard-boiled eggs, peeled and halved

2 radishes, chopped

fresh dill sprigs

85 g (3 oz/⅓ cup) sour cream

Heat the butter in a large flameproof casserole dish or stockpot, then brown the beef shin on all sides until a golden crust develops. Add the onion, carrot, celery and bay leaves to the pot and cook for a few minutes until the vegetables are starting to soften. Add 2 litres (70 fl oz/8 cups) of water with 1 teaspoon salt and the cider vinegar, bring to a simmer and cook for about an hour or until the meat is falling off the bone.

Scoop out the beef and set aside.

Add the chopped beetroot and cabbage to the broth and cook, stirring occasionally until the beetroot is tender. Purée the soup with a stick blender until smooth. Season with salt and freshly ground black pepper if desired. Shred the meat from the beef shin and return to the beetroot broth, discarding the bone.

Serve, garnished with half a boiled egg, chopped radish, chopped dill and generous spoonful of sour cream.

Indian spiced lentil and tomato soup with tadka

Spiced doesn't always mean hot, and this soup showcases a range of delicious spices brimming with anti-inflammatory properties, boosting the excellent prebiotic brain benefits of the lentils. Tadka, or tempering, is a cooking technique where whole spices are quickly roasted in oil or ghee to release their essential oils before being added to a soup or curry just before serving.

SERVES 4

1 tablespoon ghee

205 g (7¼ oz/1 cup) red lentils

1 large red (Spanish) onion, sliced

1 tablespoon ground turmeric

1 tablespoon freshly grated ginger

½ teaspoon black pepper

400 g (14 oz) tin tomatoes

1 tablespoon ghee, extra, or coconut oil

1 teaspoon cumin seeds

1 teaspoon black mustard seeds

1 teaspoon fennel seeds

70 g (2½ oz/¼ cup) plain yoghurt

handful of coriander (cilantro) leaves, to serve

Melt the ghee in a heavy-based saucepan, add the lentils and red onion and cook until the onion starts to soften, then add the turmeric, ginger and black pepper and cook for a few more moments until fragrant. Add the tinned tomatoes and 1.5 litres (52 fl oz/6 cups) of water and simmer for about 30 minutes, stirring occasionally until the lentils are tender and dissolving into the soup.

To temper the spices, heat the extra ghee or coconut oil in a small frying pan. Add the cumin, mustard seeds and fennel seeds and cook until they start to sizzle and pop and smell fragrant. Remove from the heat and stir through the soup.

To serve, ladle the soup into bowls and top with a swirl of yoghurt and fresh coriander leaves.

Roasted garlic, cauliflower and cheddar chowder

Roasting the vegetables first brings out a nutty flavour to the soup, and the gentle spices give another tasty boost. The cheese adds a bit of protein to top that off. This recipe has a bit of salt from the cheese and salt added during cooking the vegetables; it's balanced by potassium from the cauliflower, potato, onion and parsley, but if you are not used to adding salt in cooking, you can choose not to add it to this dish.

SERVES 6

1 garlic bulb

1 cauliflower, cut into small florets

2 small potatoes, peeled and chopped into roughly 2 cm (¾ inch) pieces

1 small red (Spanish) onion, roughly chopped

2 tablespoons olive oil

1 tablespoon ground turmeric

1 teaspoon ground cumin

1 teaspoon pepper

1 teaspoon salt

2 litres (70 fl oz/8 cups) vegetable stock or water

1 cup cooked chickpeas (see page 78)

50 g (1¾ oz/½ cup) grated cheddar cheese

300 ml (10½ fl oz) cream

chopped flat-leaf (Italian) parsley, to serve

crispy roasted chickpeas (see page 203), to serve

Preheat the oven to 200°C (400°F).

Wrap the whole garlic bulb in foil and set aside. The garlic is going to steam in its little package.

Put the cauliflower florets, potato and onion in a baking dish then drizzle with the olive oil and sprinkle with the turmeric, cumin, pepper and salt. Then use your hands to toss the vegetables until they are covered in golden, spiced oil. Shake the pan to even out the vegetables, nestle the foil-wrapped garlic in one corner, put the tray in the oven and roast for about 20 minutes until the cauliflower is starting to brown and the potatoes are just tender. Remove from the oven and set aside to cool slightly.

Transfer the vegetables to a large saucepan and add the stock and chickpeas. Bring to the boil over medium heat. Reduce to a simmer and cook for 5 minutes. Remove from the heat and use a stick blender to purée until smooth. Add a little extra water or stock if too thick. Return to the heat and stir through the cheddar and cream. Season with salt and pepper if desired.

Serve immediately with chopped parsley and a swirl of olive oil. Scatter with crispy roasted chickpeas.

Three-pea soup

A lively green soup full of antioxidants, anti-inflammatory benefits and great prebiotics, this is perfect for spring, when the weather's unpredictable so you want something nourishing but light.

SERVES 4

2 tablespoons butter

1 onion, chopped

3 celery stalks, chopped

2 carrots, chopped

1 tablespoon fresh thyme

2 garlic cloves, chopped

110 g (3¾ oz/½ cup) dried split peas

1.5 litres (52 fl oz/6 cups) vegetable stock or water

155 g (5½ oz/1 cup) frozen or fresh peas

Greek-style yoghurt, to serve

pea shoots or pea tops from the garden, to serve

40 g (1½ oz/¼ cup) pumpkin seeds (pepitas), toasted

handful of chopped mint, to serve

In a large heavy-based saucepan, melt the butter over medium heat, then add the onion, celery, carrots, thyme and garlic and cook until the onion is soft. Add the split peas and stir to coat, then add the stock. Bring to the boil, then reduce the heat and simmer for about 1 hour until the peas fall apart and are creamy. You may need to add more water or stock if it's too thick. Add the whole peas and cook for about 2 minutes until the peas are heated through but still bright green. Remove from the heat and use a stick blender to purée the soup until it's smooth and a lovely bright green colour.

To serve, ladle into soup bowls, add a swirl of yoghurt and top with pea shoots, then scatter with toasted pumpkin seeds and chopped mint. Sprinkle with freshly ground black pepper.

Chicken and black bean soup with coriander and lime and blue corn chips

Blue corn really is a thing, and these beautifully coloured corn chips, which can be found in the organic section of most supermarkets, have the benefit of the extra antioxidants that give the corn its blue colour. If you can't find blue corn chips you can substitute regular corn chips. Most commercially available corn chips will have added salt (check the ingredients list on the packet), so for this recipe and to keep the salt down, don't buy flavoured ones, but go for plain.

SERVES 2

2 tablespoons olive oil

1 small red (Spanish) onion, finely chopped

2 garlic cloves, crushed

small bunch of coriander (cilantro), stems finely chopped, leaves picked

2 teaspoons ground cumin

1 teaspoon ground coriander

½ teaspoon dried chilli flakes

400 g (14 oz) black beans, cooked

600 ml (21 fl oz) chicken stock

200 g (7 oz/1 cup) corn kernels

250 g (9 oz) cooked chicken, shredded

zest and juice of 2 limes

50 g (1¾ oz) crème fraîche

blue corn chips, to serve

Heat the olive oil in a large saucepan over medium heat, then add the onion and cook until softened, then add the garlic and coriander stalks and fry for 2 minutes or until fragrant.

Stir in the cumin, ground coriander and chilli and fry for a few moments more, then add the beans and stock. Increase the heat and bring to a lively simmer.

Stir the corn into the soup, simmer for 5 minutes or until the corn is tender, then add the chicken and let it heat through. Season to taste with salt and pepper and stir through the lime zest and juice.

Serve in shallow bowls, with a spoonful of crème fraîche and a scattering of coriander leaves. Crumble the corn chips over the top.

SNACKS & DRINKS

When hunger strikes at odd times, rather than reaching for something of dubious nutritional benefit, choose one of these recipes for an opportunity to give your brain a power-packed boost.

Macadamia and cauliflower hummus

What a delicious take on traditional hummus! Macadamia nuts are a bit higher in protein than the chickpeas usually used and add a lovely creaminess as well as some extra, healthy fats to this dip. If you want even more protein you could substitute some blanched almonds for some of the macadamias: it's only a subtle flavour change, and while both nuts are great protein sources, almonds have about twice the protein. The tahini adds to the protein, and that's boosted by the all-round goodness of cauliflower, topped with the anti-inflammatory flourish of the olive oil.

MAKES 1½ CUPS

60 ml (2 fl oz/¼ cup) olive oil

½ cauliflower, broken into small florets

60 g (2¼ oz/½ cup) macadamia nuts, soaked for 2 hours in warm water

1 tablespoon tahini

juice of 1 lemon

2 garlic cloves, chopped

1 teaspoon ground cumin

In a frying pan, heat 1 tablespoon of the olive oil, add the cauliflower and stir over low heat until golden brown and tender. Remove from the heat.

Drain the macadamia nuts and reserve the soaking water. Put the nuts into the bowl of a food processor, along with the cauliflower. Pulse for about 1 minute until smooth, adding some of the reserved water if the paste is too thick. Add the tahini, lemon juice, garlic and cumin and pulse again until you have a smooth paste; you don't want it too stiff so add more of the reserved water if you need to. Stir through the remaining olive oil and serve with crackers.

Roasted carrot, yoghurt and tahini dip

The lemoniness of this dip depends on the lemons you happen to find, as some have a stronger flavour than others, but it adds a great flavour balance to this dip, which is packed with antioxidants from the carrots, the anti-inflammatory benefits of extra virgin olive oil and some protein from the yoghurt and tahini.

MAKES 1½ CUPS

500 g (1 lb 2 oz) baby Dutch carrots, coloured ones if you can find them

60 ml (2 fl oz/¼ cup) olive oil, plus extra for roasting

70 g (2½ oz/¼ cup) Greek-style yoghurt

65 g (2½ oz/¼ cup) tahini

1 teaspoon ground cumin

juice and zest of 1 lemon

crackers, to serve

Preheat the oven to 180°C (350°F).

Scrub and trim the carrots and if they're thick, slice them in half lengthways, then spread them out on a baking tray, drizzle with a little extra olive oil and season with salt.

Roast in the oven until soft and starting to turn dark golden on the edges. Set aside to cool.

Put the cooled carrots into the bowl of a food processor and pulse until finely chopped. Add the yoghurt, tahini, cumin and lemon juice and zest and pulse again until combined. With the motor running, drizzle the olive oil into the carrots and process for 30–40 seconds or until the dip comes together and looks creamy and smooth.

Season to taste and serve with crackers.

Crumbed and fried boiled eggs

A protein-packed tasty snack in their own right, these eggs are best served with a selection of salad leaves, herbs and greens from the garden.

MAKES 6

7 eggs

75 g (2¾ oz/½ cup) plain (all-purpose) flour

60 g (2¼ oz/1 cup) panko breadcrumbs

20 g (¾ oz/1 cup) flat-leaf (Italian) parsley leaves, very finely chopped

½ teaspoon very finely chopped fresh rosemary leaves

35 g (1¼ oz/⅓ cup) grated parmesan cheese

500 ml (17 fl oz/2 cups) vegetable oil

Bring a medium saucepan of water to the boil, then use a slotted spoon to gently lower 6 of the eggs into the water. Boil for 5 minutes and then remove with the slotted spoon and transfer to a bowl of iced water. Let the eggs cool for 10 minutes, then carefully peel.

Season the flour with salt and pepper and put it into a shallow bowl. Beat the remaining egg in a separate small bowl. In a third bowl, mix the breadcrumbs, chopped herbs and parmesan cheese.

Carefully dredge each egg in the flour, then dip it in the beaten egg and coat it in the breadcrumb mix.

Heat the vegetable oil in a deep saucepan over medium–high heat. To test if the oil is ready, drop a pinch of breadcrumbs into the oil; if it sizzles straight away, you're ready to fry.

Using a slotted spoon, gently lower one crumbed egg into the hot oil. Deep-fry for about 30 seconds, gently turning the egg with the spoon until it is brown all over.

Drain on paper towel and continue frying the remaining crumbed eggs.

The eggs can be eaten immediately, seasoned with salt and pepper if desired, or they can be cooled then kept for up to 4 days in an airtight container in the fridge. Reheat the eggs on a small baking tray in an oven preheated to 180°C (350°F) for about 10 minutes before serving.

Crispy roasted chickpeas

A brain-healthy alternative to chips or commercial snack foods. These guys are best served straight away as they will gradually lose their crispness and become chewy as they cool. Still good, just different.

MAKES 3 CUPS

3 cups cooked chickpeas
(see page 78) or use tinned
chickpeas, rinsed and drained

2 tablespoons olive oil

½ teaspoon salt (optional)

2 tablespoons finely chopped
rosemary leaves

1 teaspoon smoked paprika

pinch of cayenne pepper

Heat the oven to 190°C (375°F).

Spread the chickpeas onto a clean tea towel (dish towel) to dry. Use paper towel to blot any excess moisture. They shouldn't look shiny, but feel dry to the touch.

Spread the chickpeas out in an even layer on a baking try. Drizzle with the olive oil and sprinkle with the salt (if using). Stir with your hands to make sure the chickpeas are evenly coated.

Roast the chickpeas for 20–30 minutes, remembering to stir them or shake the tray every 10 minutes. When the chickpeas are golden and slightly darkened, they are done. Toss the chickpeas with the rosemary and spices and serve at once.

Chewy oat and ginger bikkies

A dense, chewy biscuit with added good fats, fibre and protein from LSA, coconut and tahini. They are great plain, but chocolate and sesame seeds add extra flavour mileage. Choose chocolate with at least 70% cocoa solids (usually called extra dark) to pack in the antioxidants and keep the sugar content down.

MAKES 16 BISCUITS

120 g (4¼ oz) plain (all-purpose) flour

105 g (3½ oz/1 cup) instant oats

60 g (2¼ oz/½ cup) LSA

100 g (3½ oz/½ cup lightly packed) brown sugar

110 g (3¾ oz/½ cup) sugar

35 g (1¼ oz/½ cup) shredded coconut

45 g (1½ oz/½ cup) quinoa flakes

½ teaspoon bicarbonate of soda (baking soda)

50 g (1¾ oz) candied ginger, finely chopped

170 g (6 oz) butter

2 tablespoons golden syrup (light treacle)

135 g (4¾ oz/½ cup) tahini

½ teaspoon ground cinnamon

200 g (7 oz) dark chocolate (70% cocoa), optional

sesame seeds, for sprinkling (optional)

Preheat the oven to 180°C (350°F) and line two baking trays with baking paper.

In a large bowl, whisk the flour, oats, LSA, combined sugars, coconut and quinoa flakes and bicarbonate of soda until combined. Stir the ginger through.

In a small saucepan, melt the butter, golden syrup, tahini and cinnamon over medium heat until melted and combined.

Pour the butter mix into the dry mixture, and stir until well combined.

Drop heaped tablespoon-sized balls of dough onto the baking tray, spaced about 7 cm (2¾ inches) apart. Flatten the tops of the dough slightly and, if any edges crack, pinch them back together.

Bake for 20 minutes or until just starting to turn golden. Cool on the tray for 5 minutes (they're very soft and fragile at this point) before transferring to a wire rack to cool completely.

If desired, while the bikkies are cooling, gently heat the chocolate in a small bowl over simmering water (don't let the base of the bowl touch the water) until melted. Drizzle the melted chocolate over the bikkies and sprinkle with sesame seeds. Store the bikkies in an airtight container for up to 4 days.

Savoury coconut chips

Such a simple recipe and a great snack to have on hand: the fats in the coconut help the absorption of the turmeric.

MAKES 2 CUPS

1 teaspoon turmeric

½ teaspoon salt (optional)

pinch of cayenne pepper

freshly ground black pepper

110 g (3¾ oz/2 cups) coconut flakes

Combine the turmeric, salt (if using), cayenne and black pepper in a small bowl and set aside. Heat a large heavy-based frying pan over medium heat and add the coconut flakes. Cook the flakes, constantly stirring, for about 2–3 minutes until they start to turn golden. Remove from the heat and toss with the spice mix. Spread onto a baking tray to cool. Store in an airtight container for up to 1 week.

Spiced orange and ginger cordial

Dehydration is anathema to peak brain function so — while water is the best option most of the time — this refreshing drink with the benefits of antioxidants and spices offers a great way to boost your fluids on a hot day. Soak overnight to extract as much benefit from the spices as possible.

MAKES 4 CUPS

zest and juice of 5 oranges, reserving the juiced halves

zest and juice of 1 lemon

1 thumb-size piece of fresh ginger, grated

5 cardamom pods, smashed open

2 cinnamon sticks

5 whole cloves

2 whole star anise

200 g (7 oz) sugar

1 litre (35 fl oz/4 cups) boiling water

Combine all of the ingredients, including the juiced orange halves, in a large ceramic bowl and stir until the sugar dissolves. Cover and stand overnight to cool and for the flavours to infuse. The next day, strain the cordial through a fine sieve. Discard the solids. Pour the cordial into a sterile glass bottle or large jar and store in the fridge.

To serve, mix 1 part cordial to 4 parts chilled water, still or sparkling, or dilute to taste.

Turmeric latte (golden milk)

Turmeric offers both antioxidant and anti-inflammatory benefits for your brain, but is best absorbed when eaten along with some fat, while pepper is also thought to help. The full-cream milk suggested in this recipe is therefore important to help its absorption. This drink is not only delicious, but is an easy way to get the benefits of turmeric daily. Molasses has very small amounts of some minerals not found in granulated sugar, but if it's too strongly flavoured for you, try golden syrup, which still provides some, though not as much, of those minerals. Makes a perfect night cap.

SERVES 2

500 ml (17 fl oz/2 cups) full-cream milk

1 teaspoon molasses or golden syrup (light treacle)

1 teaspoon honey

1 teaspoon ground turmeric

½ teaspoon ground cinnamon

¼ teaspoon ground ginger

pinch of pepper

In a small saucepan, gently heat the milk, molasses and honey until bubbles appear around the edge of the saucepan, but do not boil. Remove from the heat and add the spices, whisking until combined. Serve at once.

TURMERIC SPICE MIXTURE

You can also make a large batch of this spice mixture so it's ready to add to warm milk at any time. A trip to the health-food store might be your best bet to buy the spices in bulk.

Mix together ¼ cup of ground turmeric, 1½ tablespoons of ground cinnamon, 1 teaspoon of freshly ground black pepper and 1 tablespoon of ground ginger. Store in an airtight container for up to 12 months.

Super hot chocolate

This warming sweet drink gives the antioxidant benefits of cocoa or raw cacao (see page 70 for more information about the difference between the two).

MAKES 1 CUP

2 tablespoons unsweetened cocoa powder (or use raw cacao powder, although the flavour will be different)

1 teaspoon ground cinnamon

60 ml (2 fl oz/¼ cup) boiling water

1 tablespoon golden syrup (light treacle) or maple syrup

pinch of cayenne pepper (optional)

185 ml (6 fl oz/¾ cup) milk

In a cup, combine cocoa, cinnamon and cayenne pepper (if using) then add the boiling water. Stir in the golden syrup until the syrup has dissolved. Top up with warm milk and serve immediately.

FRUIT & SWEET THINGS

These recipes can be used as antioxidant-rich, fibre-boosted and higher-protein extras when the lure of a sweeter treat might be the way to encourage eating. Read more about sugar on page 58 and see Chapter 8 for tips on balancing your diet.

Spelt carrot, walnut and coconut cake

Try to find heirloom carrots: purple, red or yellow will yield a greater variety of antioxidants in this nutritious cake, which means you can have an extra slice! It's also packed with bonus ingredients: walnuts and LSA for omega–3; spices, coconut, raisins and eggs for potassium, fibre and protein.

SERVES 8

100 g (3½ oz) sugar

80 g (2¾ oz) brown sugar

80 ml (2½ fl oz/⅓ cup) rice bran oil

2 tablespoons orange juice

zest of 1 orange

1 teaspoon natural vanilla extract

2 large eggs

465 g (1 lb ½ oz/3 cups) carrots, grated (about six carrots)

50 g (1¾ oz/½ cup) walnuts, chopped

20 g (¾ oz/¼ cup) shredded coconut

45 g (1½ oz/¼ cup) sultanas (golden raisins)

90 g (3¼ oz) plain (all-purpose) spelt flour

1 teaspoon baking powder

½ teaspoon bicarbonate of soda (baking soda)

½ teaspoon ground allspice

1 teaspoon ground cinnamon

½ teaspoon salt

2 tablespoons LSA

Greek-style yoghurt, to serve

Preheat the oven to 180°C (350°F). Grease and line a 20 cm (8 inch) cake tin with baking paper.

In a large mixing bowl, combine the sugars, rice bran oil, orange juice, zest, vanilla and the eggs. Stir until nice and smooth. Mix in the carrots, walnuts, coconut and sultanas.

In a second mixing bowl, whisk together the flour, baking powder, bicarbonate of soda, spices, salt and the LSA.

Add the dry ingredients to the wet mix and stir until well combined.

Pour the batter into the prepared cake tin and bake for 40–45 minutes until a skewer inserted into the cake comes out clean.

Cool in the tin for 10 minutes before turning out onto a wire rack to cool.

Serve with a dollop of Greek-style yoghurt.

Almond teacake with raspberries

A twist on the traditional teacake: this one is made by replacing some flour with almond meal to add extra protein and vitamin E, and includes coconut and raspberries for their fibre and antioxidants.

SERVES 8–10

120 g (4¼ oz) butter, softened

200 g (7 oz) sugar

1 tablespoon golden syrup (light treacle)

2 eggs, beaten

120 g (4¼ oz) plain (all-purpose) spelt flour

100 g (3½ oz/1 cup) almond meal

1 tablespoon ground cinnamon

1¼ teaspoons baking powder

125 g (4½ oz) yoghurt

TOPPING

3 tablespoons brown sugar

125 g (4½ oz/1 cup) raspberries, fresh or frozen

80 g (2¾ oz/½ cup) almonds, chopped

35 g (1¼ oz/½ cup) shredded coconut

1 teaspoon ground cinnamon

Preheat the oven to 180°C (350°F). Grease and line a 11 x 21 cm (4¼ x 8¼ inch) loaf tin with baking paper.

Using a stand mixer, cream the butter, sugar and golden syrup until pale. Add the eggs and beat well to combine.

Sift together the flour, almond meal, cinnamon and baking powder. Gently fold the flour mixture into the wet ingredients, then add the yoghurt.

Pour into the prepared tin and bake for 20 minutes.

Just before the cake is finished, make the topping. Combine all of the ingredients in a small bowl and mix well.

Carefully remove the cake from the oven and cover the top with the raspberry mixture.

Return to the oven and cook for a further 15 minutes or until a cake tester comes out clean.

Cool in the tin for 10 minutes, then remove from tin and transfer to a wire rack to cool completely.

Blackcurrant ice cream

This is the simplest ice-cream recipe in the world and it doesn't need an ice cream machine. Blackcurrants aren't the easiest fruit to track down, unless you know someone who grows them or grow them yourself, but they are a deep purple, luscious-flavoured fruit filled with antioxidants and worth seeking out. If you can't get your hands on any, swap for another dark purple fruit such as blood plums, blueberries or blackberries. Treat berries the same way as the currants, but, unless you want to avoid the seeds, you don't need to push them through a sieve. Blackcurrants have a really tough skin that's best taken out of the equation. Alternatively, roast halved blood plums and fold those tart, dusky fruits through the ice cream.

SERVES 6

3 large eggs, separated

1 tablespoon natural vanilla extract

500 ml (17 fl oz/2 cups) thin (pouring) cream

100 g (3½ oz) pure icing (confectioners') sugar

500 g (1 lb 2 oz) blackcurrants or other dark purple fruit

3 large thyme sprigs

In a medium bowl, whisk the eggwhites until soft peaks form. In another bowl, mix the egg yolks and vanilla extract until thickened and pale. Fold the eggwhites into the yolk mixture.

Beat the cream and icing sugar together in another bowl until soft and billowy. Lightly fold the cream into the egg mixture with a metal spoon until combined.

Pour into a shallow container that will fit in your freezer and freeze for 1 hour.

While the ice cream freezes, heat the blackcurrants and thyme sprigs in a little water. When soft, remove from the heat and push through a sieve. Discard the pulp and thyme.

You should have a thick blackcurrant sauce; set this aside to cool while the ice cream begins to freeze. When it's cool, transfer it to the freezer to chill quickly.

After the ice cream has been in the freezer for 1 hour, remove and fold through the cold blackcurrant sauce to make ripples, then return it to the freezer for another 2 hours before serving.

Rich egg custard with roasted rhubarb and nut crumble

Rhubarb and custard is such a classic pairing, but adding the nut crumble boosts the nutritional profile of this dessert. There are three elements to this recipe, and they're all delicious enough to stand alone and be used in different meals. This custard, which is the real sort, made with protein-rich eggs, can be eaten with any dessert, such as the blueberry buckle (see page 230) or the fig tart (see page 226), or you can also serve it with fresh fruit. The nut crumble recipe makes a big batch: you'll have some left over and it's worth storing it in an airtight container to serve with yoghurt or stewed fruit, or simply to eat by the handful as a snack. The rhubarb can be served on your porridge, or eaten with yoghurt and a drizzle of honey.

SERVES 4

CUSTARD

375 ml (13 fl oz/1½ cups) thin (pouring) cream

¼ teaspoon freshly grated nutmeg

½ vanilla bean, seeds scraped

5 large egg yolks

55 g (2 oz/¼ cup) sugar

RHUBARB

1 bunch of rhubarb

60 g (2¼ oz/⅓ cup) brown sugar

juice and zest of 1 orange

To make the custard, put the cream in a small saucepan over medium heat and add the nutmegand vanilla. Bring this to just below a simmer; you'll see little bubbles forming around the edge, that's when to take it off the heat.

In a small bowl, whisk the egg yolks and sugar. Try not to make it foamy, you're just combining the two. Add a little of the cream to the yolks while whisking, then gradually pour in about half of the cream while whisking constantly. Return this mixture to the saucepan and, using a wooden spoon, cook for 3–4 minutes over medium–low heat, stirring constantly to make sure it doesn't catch on the bottom, until it thickens enough to coat the back of the spoon. Strain into a bowl, and either serve straight away or allow to cool before covering and storing in the fridge.

To roast the rhubarb, preheat the oven to 180°C (350°F).

Wash the rhubarb, cut off any dry edges or leaves, then cut into 5 cm (2 inch) pieces. Spread on a baking tray and sprinkle with the brown sugar, orange juice and zest. Cover with foil and roast for 25–30 minutes until tender.

To make the nut crumble, preheat the oven to 180°C (350°F) and line a large baking tray with baking paper.

NUT CRUMBLE

75 g (2¾ oz/½ cup) macadamia nuts

60 g (2¼ oz/½ cup) walnuts

80 g (2¾ oz/½ cup) almonds

75 g (2¾ oz/½ cup) hazelnuts (filberts)

1 tablespoon ground cinnamon

85 g (3 oz/1½ cups) coconut flakes

50 g (1¾ oz) butter

1 tablespoon golden syrup (light treacle) or honey

Put the combined nuts and cinnamon into a food processor and pulse once or twice until nuts are coarsely chopped. Transfer to a large bowl then add the coconut. Season with salt if desired.

In a small saucepan, melt the butter with the golden syrup. Pour the melted butter mixture over the nut mixture and use your hands or a spoon to stir it around so everything's well coated. Spread out the mixture on the prepared baking tray so it's nice and even.

Bake for 10 minutes. Remove from the oven, stir the nuts up a bit and return to the oven for another 5–10 minutes until they turn a lovely tan colour and have a nutty smell. Remove from the oven and allow to cool, then store in an airtight container for up to 2 weeks.

Serve the rhubarb in a bowl with nut crumble on top. Pour the custard over.

Orange and golden syrup dumplings with pecans

A classic comfort dish, in this recipe we add nuts for protein and antioxidants, some ginger for its anti-inflammatory properties, and orange zest. Still nostalgic, but a little more brainy. Serve with rich egg custard (see page 222) or a little cream if you fancy.

SERVES 4

150 g (5½ oz/1 cup) self-raising flour

1 tablespoon ground ginger

2 tablespoons butter, chilled and cubed, plus 30 g (1 oz) extra

45 g (1½ oz/⅓ cup) pecan nuts, roughly chopped

2 tablespoons milk

1 egg, beaten

120 g (4¼ oz) brown sugar

zest and juice of 2 oranges

90 g (3¼ oz/¼ cup) golden syrup (light treacle)

Sift the flour and ginger into a large bowl. Add the butter and rub between your fingertips until the mixture resembles breadcrumbs. Stir in the pecans. Make a well in the centre of the flour mixture and add the milk and egg. Use a butter knife to mix until well combined. Divide into eight equal portions, and roll each portion into a ball using your hands.

In a large saucepan with a well-fitting lid, melt the sugar, extra butter, orange zest and juice and golden syrup over low heat, until the sugar dissolves. You'll need to stir it occasionally. Increase the heat to medium–high and bring to the boil. Lower the heat and carefully place the dumplings into the syrup.

Reduce the heat to medium–low, cover with the lid and cook for 6–7 minutes until a skewer inserted into the centre of the dumplings comes out clean. Turn the dumplings in syrup so they're all covered in the sauce. Spoon the dumplings and syrup into serving bowls and top with custard or even a generous dollop of cream. Serve immediately.

Fig and apricot tart with cardamom maple cream

This rustic tart is pretty easy to make. The pastry has a mix of LSA which adds anti-inflammatory omega-3s as well as great fibre. You can make it in summer using fresh figs and apricots, but using dried fruit means you can make it any time of the year. You could also swap the figs and apricots for fresh blueberries when in season. When using fresh fruit, you don't need to cook it first, just place the fruit on the ricotta filling.

SERVES 8

185 g (6½ oz/1¼ cups) plain (all-purpose) flour

30 g (1 oz/¼ cup) icing (confectioners') sugar mixture

½ teaspoon ground cinnamon

30 g (1 oz/¼ cup) LSA

125 g (4½ oz) butter, chilled and chopped

50 g (1¾ oz/½ cup) slivered almonds

1 egg yolk, beaten, plus 1 extra beaten egg yolk for brushing

FRUIT FILLING

500 ml (17 fl oz/2 cups) orange juice

155 g (5½ oz/1 cup) dried apricots

185 g (6½ oz/1 cup) dried figs, halved lengthways

60 g (2¼ oz) butter, chopped

110 g (3¾ oz/½ cup) caster (superfine) sugar

To make the pastry, pulse the flour, icing sugar, cinnamon, LSA and butter in the bowl of a food processor for about 2 minutes until the mixture resembles fine breadcrumbs. Add the egg yolk and process until the dough comes together in a ball. Turn out onto a lightly floured surface. Knead quickly until just smooth. Shape into a disc, smoothing any cracks that appear around the edges. Cover with plastic wrap and chill in the fridge for 30 minutes.

Preheat the oven to 180°C (350°F). Line a baking tray with baking paper.

To make the fruit filling, combine the orange juice, apricots, figs, butter and sugar in a medium saucepan. Bring to the boil, then reduce the heat and simmer, uncovered, for 4–5 minutes until the fruit is plump and tender. Drain and set aside.

Meanwhile, in a small bowl, combine the ricotta cheese, egg, lemon juice, zest, vanilla seeds and sugar. Stir until all the ingredients are smooth.

To assemble the tart, remove the pastry from the fridge and roll it out on a lightly floured surface. You're aiming for a circle about 30 cm (12 inches) in diameter or about 5 mm (¼ inch) thick.

RICOTTA FILLING

115 g (4 oz/½ cup) ricotta cheese

1 egg, beaten

1 tablespoon lemon juice

zest of 1 lemon

1 vanilla bean, split lengthways, seeds scraped

2 tablespoons brown sugar

CARDAMOM MAPLE CREAM

250 ml (9 fl oz/1 cup) thin (pouring) cream

2 tablespoons maple syrup

½ teaspoon ground cardamom

Lay the pastry on the prepared baking tray. Smear the ricotta mixture in a circle on the pastry, leaving a rim of about 3 cm (1¼ inches) clear around the edge. Place the figs and the apricots on top. Then fold over about 2 cm (¾ inch) around the edge of the pastry to make a lip. Scatter the slivered almonds on top. Brush the exposed pastry with the extra beaten egg yolk, then bake for 30 minutes or until golden. Allow to cool.

To make the cardamom maple cream, combine all of the ingredients in a medium bowl and beat until soft peaks form. Serve the tart at room temperature with the cardamom maple cream.

Peach trifle

You can use any fruit you like for this recipe: peaches, apricots, nectarines or plums are all delicious roasted in this way. The granola recipe makes a big batch and any extra can be stored in an airtight container.

SERVES 4

4 large peaches

45 g (1½ oz/¼ cup lightly packed) brown sugar

40 g (1½ oz) butter, chopped

GRANOLA

60 g (2¼ oz) butter

2 tablespoons ground cinnamon

1 teaspoon ground ginger

115 g (4 oz/⅓ cup) golden syrup (light treacle)

200 g (7 oz/2 cups) rolled (porridge) oats

40 g (1½ oz/¼ cup) sesame seeds

75 g (2¾ oz/½ cup) pumpkin seeds (pepitas)

2 tablespoons poppy seeds

80 g (2¾ oz/½ cup) almonds

75 g (2¾ oz/½ cup) macadamias, chopped

35 g (1¼ oz/½ cup) shredded coconut

VANILLA YOGHURT

500 g (1 lb 2 oz) Greek-style yoghurt

1 teaspoon natural vanilla extract

2 teaspoons honey

Preheat the oven to 180°C (350°F) then start on the granola.

In a small saucepan, melt the butter, spices and golden syrup until combined. In a large bowl, combine the oats, sesame, pumpkin and poppy seeds, almonds, macadamia nuts and coconut and pour the melted butter mixture over the top. Mix well to combine. Tip onto a baking sheet and spread the mixture out evenly. Cook in the oven for about 25 minutes until dry, golden and crisp. Remove from the oven and allow to cool.

Halve the peaches and discard the stones, then slice and arrange on a baking tray. Sprinkle the brown sugar and scatter the butter over the slices and roast for 20 minutes or until starting to brown at the edges. Remove from the oven and allow to cool.

To make the vanilla yoghurt, combine all of the ingredients in a small bowl.

In four small glasses, layer the fruit, yoghurt and granola, starting with the peaches, followed by the yoghurt, then the granola, then repeat the layers. Chill in the fridge for 30 minutes before serving.

Blueberry buckle

A blueberry buckle is an old-fashioned American cake with a streusel topping that 'buckles' as it cooks. We've given this classic a bit of a healthy makeover with wholemeal spelt flour and hazelnuts.

SERVES 8

150 g (5½ oz/1 cup) wholemeal spelt flour, or regular wholemeal (whole-wheat) flour

2 teaspoons baking powder

110 g (3¾ oz/½ cup) sugar

50 g (1¾ oz) LSA

60 g (2¼ oz) butter, melted

1 teaspoon natural vanilla extract

2 eggs, lightly beaten

100 g (3½ oz) yoghurt

465 g (1 lb ¼ oz/3 cups) fresh or frozen blueberries

CRUMBLE TOPPING

30 g (1 oz/¼ cup) finely chopped hazelnuts (filberts)

35 g (1¼ oz/¼ cup) self-raising flour

55 g (2 oz/¼ cup) raw sugar

1 teaspoon ground cinnamon

50 g (1¾ oz) butter

Preheat the oven to 170°C (325°F). Grease a 22 cm (8½ inch) round cake tin with melted butter, line with baking paper and set aside.

To make the crumble topping, mix together the hazelnuts, sugar and cinnamon in a small bowl. Add the butter and stir until crumbly: you want quite large crumbs, about the size of a pea. Set aside.

In a large bowl, sift together the spelt flour, baking powder and season with salt if desired. Add the sugar and LSA and stir through. In a separate bowl, whisk together the melted butter, vanilla, eggs and yoghurt. Add the butter mixture to the dry ingredients and quickly stir until well combined. Transfer the batter to the prepared cake tin, then pile the blueberries on the top. Push them lightly into the batter so you have a relatively smooth surface. Spread the crumble topping over the blueberries; you may have a few gaps, but that's okay. Bake for 45–50 minutes or until a skewer inserted in the centre comes out clean.

Let cool and serve.

Chocolate mousse with cardamom

Dark chocolate is usually made from roasted cacao beans and is a combination of the cocoa solids and varying amounts of cocoa butter. The 70% cocoa specified in this recipe is high in cocoa solids, so has a strong flavour and is also high in antioxidants. That actually makes it quite good for you! The addition of a little cardamom in the mix and a few pistachios adds to the deliciousness.

SERVES 6

100 ml (3½ fl oz) thin (pouring) cream

8 cardamom pods, smashed

1 tablespoon golden syrup (light treacle)

200 g (7 oz) dark chocolate (70% cocoa solids), chopped

4 egg yolks

6 eggwhites

2 teaspoons sugar

whipped cream, chopped pistachios and berries (optional), to serve

Put the cream, cardamom pods and golden syrup in a small saucepan and gently heat until it just begins to come to the boil. Set aside to cool.

Put the chocolate in a heatproof bowl set over a saucepan of simmering water (don't let the base of the bowl touch the water). Heat until the chocolate has melted and turned smooth and silky.

Strain the cooled cream into the chocolate and stir to combine. Add the egg yolks, beating until well combined. It might start to look a bit grainy, but that's okay.

In a separate bowl, beat the eggwhites until soft peaks form. Add the sugar and continue to whip until stiff. Fold about a quarter of the eggwhite mixture into the chocolate mixture, using a metal spoon. Fold in the remaining eggwhite mixture until combined and there are no visible traces of eggwhite. Spoon the mousse into 6 small glasses. Place the glasses in the fridge to set for at least 4 hours or overnight.

Top with a little whipped cream and some chopped pistachios. If berries are in season, a few scattered on top would make a nice addition, but it's pretty good as it is.

Index

Acknowledgments

I'm immensely grateful for this book, the culmination of a long and often challenging journey. I started with a driving passion to create awareness of the unique nutritional needs of body and brain ageing. My first two books, *Eat To Cheat Ageing* and *Eat To Cheat Dementia* were self-published by necessity, but for this fabulous, beautiful book I thank Michelle Crawford, Jane Morrow and the wonderful Murdoch team.

It wouldn't exist though without those who were with me from the start and they deserve the accolades. Geriatrician ('world's best'!) Dr Peter Lipski for his inspiration and encouragement — he tried, frustratingly unsuccessfully, for decades to make governments and policymakers understand all I now say! To my wonderful family: Craig and Jackson managed to live with this obsessed woman through this whole process; they also, along with Angus and Nell, encouraged, supported and endured my laments or exaltations. To my friends, especially Cathie and John, doctors offering unwavering support, editing advice, perspectives on medications and much more; those with the faith to back me early on, especially my dad, Graeme and the stars who crowdfunded the second book. There are many more but the last thanks go to my mum, Helen, who has never wavered in her belief that I will get to this place and beyond.

NGAIRE

It was a dream brief to write the recipes for this book: loads of colourful vegetables, big on spices, nuts and pulses with a healthy dose of fats. It's just the way I like to eat. Thank you, Ngaire, for asking me to be a part of it.

Heartfelt thanks to Alan Benson for the beautiful photos, your patience and your puns.

Also a big shout out to Kellie McChesney, for her usual grace and good humour, whose extraordinary organisational skills came to the fore with a challenging photography schedule; Franca Zingler, who worked her dazzling magic on many of the cake and biscuit recipes and photos; and Nisha De Jong, turmeric queen, for sharing generously her incredible knowledge of spices and other ingredients too numerous to mention.

The folk at Murdoch: Jane Morrow for asking me to be a part of this great project, to Emma Hutchinson, book wrangler extraordinaire, and Melody Lord for your keen eye and patience, and the design team.

Lastly thank you to my darling family, Leo, Elsa and Hugo, for letting the hordes raid our house for another photoshoot, for eating more salmon than is probably healthy, and for giving me the space and support, in equal measure, to write this book.

MICHELLE

Published in 2017 by Murdoch Books, an imprint of Allen & Unwin

Murdoch Books Australia
83 Alexander Street
Crows Nest NSW 2065
Phone: +61 (0) 2 8425 0100
Fax: +61 (0) 2 9906 2218
murdochbooks.com.au
info@murdochbooks.com.au

Murdoch Books UK
Ormond House
26–27 Boswell Street
London WC1N 3JZ
Phone: +44 (0) 20 8785 5995
murdochbooks.co.uk
info@murdochbooks.co.uk

For Corporate Orders & Custom Publishing, contact our Business
Development Team at salesenquiries@murdochbooks.com.au.

Publisher: Jane Morrow
Editorial Manager: Emma Hutchinson
Design Manager: Hugh Ford
Project Editor: Melody Lord
Designer: Susanne Geppert
Photographer: Alan Benson
Recipe Development and Stylist: Michelle Crawford
Production Manager: Lou Playfair

A cataloguing-in-publication entry is available from the catalogue
of the National Library of Australia at nla.gov.au.

ISBN 978 1 76052 254 4 Australia
ISBN 978 1 76052 754 9 UK

A catalogue record for this book is available from the British Library.

Colour reproduction by Splitting Image Colour Studio Pty Ltd, Clayton, Victoria
Printed by 1010 Printing International Limited, China

IMPORTANT: Those who might be at risk from the effects of salmonella poisoning (the elderly, pregnant women,
young children and those suffering from immune deficiency diseases) should consult their doctor with any concerns
about eating raw eggs.

OVEN GUIDE: You may find cooking times vary depending on the oven you are using. For fan-forced ovens,
as a general rule, set the oven temperature to 20°C (35°F) lower than indicated in the recipe.

MEASURES GUIDE: We have used 20 ml (4 teaspoon) tablespoon measures. If you are using a 15 ml (3 teaspoon)
tablespoon add an extra teaspoon of the ingredient for each tablespoon specified.

DISCLAIMER: The content presented in this book is meant for inspiration and informational purposes only.
The purchaser of this book understands that the information contained within this book is not intended to replace
medical advice or meant to be relied upon to treat, cure, or prevent any disease, illness, or medical condition. It is
understood that you will seek full medical clearance by a licensed physician before making any changes mentioned in this
book. The author and publisher claim no responsibility to any person or entity for any liability, loss, or damage caused or
alleged to be caused directly or indirectly as a result of the use, application, or interpretation of the material in this book.